THE
TOMB-BUILDERS
OF THE
PHARAOHS

THE
TOMB-BUILDERS
OF THE
PHARAOHS

MORRIS BIERBRIER

The American University in Cairo Press
Cairo   New York

1 Frontispiece *Statue of the workman Pendua and his wife. The statue is inscribed with the names of their many children.*

This paperback edition published in 2016 by
The American University in Cairo Press
113 Sharia Kasr el Aini, Cairo, Egypt
420 Fifth Avenue, New York, NY 10018
www.aucpress.com

Exclusive distribution outside Egypt and North America by I.B.Tauris & Co Ltd., 6 Salem Road, London, W4 2BU

Dar el Kutub No. 14301/15
ISBN 978 977 416 746 1

Dar el Kutub Cataloging-in-Publication Data

Bierbrier, Morris
          The Tomb-Builders of the Pharaohs / Morris Bierbrier. —Cairo:
    The American University in Cairo Press, 2016
          p.   cm.
          ISBN 978 977 416 746 1
          Deir el-Medina Site—Egypt
          Tombs—Egypt
          432.014

1 2 3 4 5   20 19 18 17 16

Designed by Tim Higgins
Printed in Egypt

Contents

Preface

I wish to thank first and foremost Professor J. M. Janssen and Dr R. Demarée who read the manuscript of this study in draft and made many useful observations, although the final result is entirely my responsibility. I also wish to express my gratitude to Mr T. G. H. James, Keeper of the Department of Egyptian Antiquities, British Museum for his encouragement and assistance. Special thanks are due to Mrs M. Černý and her daughter Mrs A. Allott, who have allowed the author to base some of the translations which appear in this work on the original translations of the late Professor Černý and also kindly supplied private photographs. Again responsibility for the final version of all translations in the text rests with the author. For the prompt supply of photographs and permission to use them in this book, I am indebted to Dr L. Bell and Mr J. Larson, of the Oriental Institute, The University of Chicago; Miss J. Bourriau of the Fitzwilliam Museum, Cambridge; Mr E. Brovarski of the Museum of Fine Arts, Boston; Professor S. Curto of the Museo Egizio, Turin; Dr A. David of the Manchester Museum; His Grace the Duke of Hamilton; Mr P. Henchy of The Chester Beatty Library; Dr C. Lilyquist of The Metropolitan Museum of Art, New York; Mr L. Limme of the Musées royaux d'Art et d'Histoire; Miss R. Moss; Dr and Mrs Munro of the Kestner Museum, Hanover; Miss H. Murray and Dr J. Málek of the Griffith Institute, Ashmolean Museum, Oxford; Mr T. Pattie and the British Library Board; Dr A. J. Spencer; Professor J. Vercoutter of Institut français d'Archéologie orientale du Caire; Dr H. Whitehouse of the Ashmolean Museum; and last, but not least, the Photographic Service of the British Museum. I would also like to thank Mrs C. Barratt for the drawings which appear in the text.

7

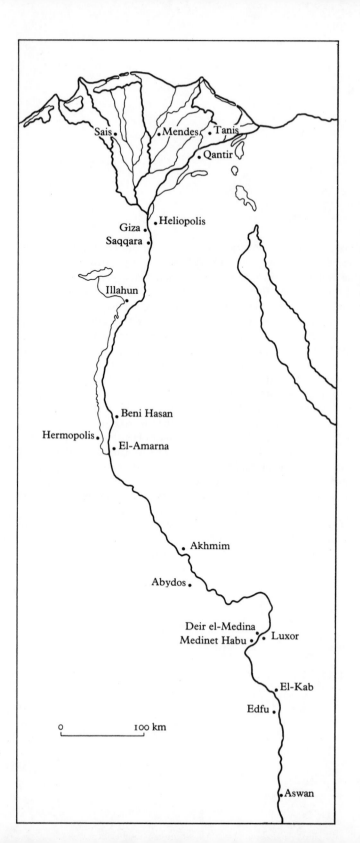

Sais •   • Mendes • Tanis

• Qantir

Giza • • Heliopolis
Saqqara •

Illahun •

• Beni Hasan

Hermopolis • • El-Amarna

• Akhmim

Abydos •

Deir el-Medina •
Medinet Habu • • Luxor

• El-Kab

Edfu •

0   100 km

• Aswan

1 The Royal Tombs

MUCH OF WHAT WE KNOW of ancient Egypt comes to us from royal inscriptions, from the tombs of the Pharaohs, and from the monuments of officials. However, in one particular village, Deir el-Medina, which was the home of a very special band of workmen, the men who built the tombs of the Pharaohs in the Valley of the Kings, it is possible to reconstruct the daily life of these ancient Egyptians. Contrary to popular belief, the workmen who constructed the tombs in the Valley of the Kings were not slaves, nor were they put to death on completion of the task to preserve the inviolability of the site, as the existence of their village at Deir el-Medina amply proves. In fact, they were a highly skilled community of craftsmen who passed their expertise on from father to son. Excavations at Deir el-Medina have yielded huge quantities of official records, literary texts, private letters and simple drawings. Thus the private delights and public disputes of the people of Deir el-Medina are laid bare before the inquisitive gaze of the modern scholar.

The very existence of a village whose whole *raison d'être* was the building of the tombs of pharaohs speaks of the ancient Egyptians' concern with the after-life. Perhaps the most visible reminders of this preoccupation are the great pyramids which were constructed to house the mortal remains of the kings. An understanding of the ancient Egyptians' enjoyment of life is an essential background to understanding their attitudes towards death. For all their seeming obsession with death, the Egyptians were not a morbid race, concerned only with death's mysteries. On the contrary, they loved life and so attempted to perpetuate its joys after death. Many of the objects which the dead person had possessed in life accompanied him to the grave for use in the hereafter, and activities in which he had participated while alive and which he hoped to enjoy again after death were depicted in his tomb. Death was thought of as being merely a continuation of life. Early in their history the Egyptians came to believe that the survival of the spirit in the after-life depended upon the survival of the body of the deceased. Thus the art of mummification was evolved to ensure that the body would remain intact in its tomb, surrounded by its possessions, for all eternity.

The Royal Tombs

The most lavish tomb in the land would naturally be accorded to the most important individual in the land – the ruler, who in Egypt was regarded as a son of the sun-god and a divinity in his own right. (The name 'pharaoh', which was at first applied only to the royal household, did not become a title of the king until later times.) During the early dynasties the royal tombs, built in the sacred city of Abydos, did not vary much in style from the rectangular mud-brick tombs of the nobles. However, towards the beginning of the Third Dynasty (c. 2660 BC) the vizier, or prime minister, Imhotep, designed for his master Djoser the great step-pyramid at Saqqara. This example was followed by the remaining rulers of this dynasty, although none has remained intact. During the next dynasty the step-pyramid was transformed into a true pyramid with a pyramidion, or capstone, at the apex, and it was in this form that royal tombs were to be built for over a thousand years.

The pyramid did not stand alone, but was part of a great complex which consisted of a valley temple at the water's edge where the royal funeral procession disembarked, a causeway which led up from the cultivation to the edge of the desert where the pyramid was built, and the pyramid itself; beside the pyramid were a mortuary temple, where prayers were destined to be offered to the deceased king in perpetuity, and other subsidiary buildings and magazines. Each new reign witnessed the construction of a new complex, but these were rarely completed before the demise of the ruler led to his hasty burial in what was ready of his eternal home. Interest then turned to the new tomb to be built. The pyramids at Giza represent the high point of pyramid construction but are far from being the sole examples of this art. In the Fifth and Sixth Dynasties the decline in resources and manpower at the disposal of the Crown meant that pyramids were built with rubble cores and only an outer casing of stone. The inner walls were now inscribed with prayers for the deceased king – the famous pyramid texts.

Just how these pyramids were built has long excited popular imagination. The Greek legend that one small pyramid was built from stones exacted by the amorous daughter of Khufu from her clients as payment is the least plausible explanation. It has been overlooked that the local administrators of Egypt were well accustomed to controlling and managing large numbers of workmen. The exact details are lacking, as documents of this early period are scanty, but the broad essentials can be pieced together from later evidence. The survival of Egypt depended upon the proper use of the flood waters of the Nile for irrigation. The early rulers and their local bureaucracy owed their power in part to the need to organize the population to construct and keep in repair the irrigation canals which channelled the flood waters to the fields. Every Egyptian citizen was in theory required to lend a hand in this effort and had to provide the state with a certain number of days of labour. This form of

2 *The Giza Pyramids of the Fourth Dynasty. These are the largest and most elaborate in a series of over forty-five pyramids, beginning with the step-pyramid of Djoser of the Third Dynasty (c. 2660 BC) and continuing into the Thirteenth Dynasty (c. 1750 BC). Later pyramids were built more economically with rubble cores and stone facing blocks.*

work tax is usually known as corvée labour. Naturally, the brunt of the conscription fell on the peasants, who formed the bulk of the population, while others evaded their duty by producing substitutes or payment to the appropriate authorities. Even in death the Egyptians believed that their spirits might be called upon to provide corvée labour in the next world and so most burials were provided with servant-figures, or *shabtis*, who would do the work instead of the owner.

The experience gained in irrigation works was soon extended to the construction of temples and tombs. Thus by the time the Great Pyramid

3 *Limestone* shabtis *of the workmen Irynufer, Djehutyhermaktef and the scribe Kenherkhepeshef. The prayers on the figures are to ensure that these servant-figures do any work required of their deceased masters in the after-life.*

was built the authorities had had several hundred years of experience in the use of human resources. The organization of manpower would have been fairly straightforward. During the time of the Nile flood, when the land would have been covered with water and unfit for agriculture, the farmers could be conscripted to work on the royal pyramid complex. Indeed, the archaeologist Flinders Petrie claimed that he had uncovered traces near Giza of the barracks in which such labourers had been housed. The size of the work-force would vary as individuals' terms of corvée ended or men were needed elsewhere. It cannot be emphasized too strongly that these men were not slaves but only temporary conscripts. Apart from domestic servants, slavery did not exist on a large scale in Egypt: corvée labour made its use unnecessary. Even the Hebrews in the Bible, who lived in Egypt over a thousand years after the pyramid age, were not slaves in the modern sense of the word. Slaves are the personal property of their master and have no rights or families, but the Hebrews had their own homes in Goshen and their own families. They were thus only providing the corvée labour for which any Egyptian subject was due, although in their case pharaoh seems to have demanded greater services than was normally imposed.

While the bulk of the work-force was made up of conscripted peasants, there obviously must have been a core of professional craftsmen and architects who were responsible for the detailed workmanship in the pyramid. No evidence survives from the Old Kingdom on the organization of these men. The modern legend that those who knew the secrets of the pyramid were killed to ensure the safety of the buried ruler is baseless. Only in the earliest period of Egyptian history (*c.* 3000 BC) is there evidence that the ruler of Egypt was accompanied into the next life by his servants. In any case, these servants were his domestic staff and not the builders of his tomb. Such practices were soon abandoned and would have been regarded with horror by the civilized rulers of the Fourth Dynasty. Besides, the architects and craftsmen were much too valuable to have been sacrificed. The new ruler also desired a pyramid complex, and quickly. The construction team would hurriedly finish off the old tomb and immediately commence work on the new. Each king knew that as much as possible of his tomb must be completed in his own life-time since his successor would naturally concentrate on building his own tomb and not on that of his predecessor.

The pyramid remained the ideal design for royal burials for over a thousand years, although rulers occasionally had to resort to modified forms in times of political uncertainty. The rulers of the Eleventh Dynasty at Thebes were buried in rock-cut cliff-tombs with adjoining temples and possibly also with pyramidal superstructures. The powerful kings of the Twelfth Dynasty reverted to the traditional design. In the Faiyum at Illahun, sometimes also known as Kahun, archaeologists have excavated a village which seems to have been founded for the construction of the pyramid of Senwosret II (*c.* 1897–1878 BC) nearby. It seems that Illahun originally housed the royal workmen who built the pyramid, but later became the residence of the priests and administrators who served the funerary cult of the deceased king. This is the earliest of the purpose-built workmen's villages established for work on royal projects for which we have firm evidence, although it is possible that such communities had existed even earlier. The houses in the village are laid out in a strict pattern with several houses in separate blocks. The houses in the main part of town were constructed of mud-brick with wooden roof beams and door-frames. These houses comprised four or more rooms on the ground floor plus a staircase to the roof, which would have been used as a terrace. The walls were plastered and sometimes covered in painted reliefs. Access to the street was through the one doorway. A number of houses had storage cellars, but infant burials have been discovered under the floors of others. Larger and more imposing residences, with colonnaded halls, have been found in other parts of the town and presumably belonged to high officials. Many objects for everyday use have been recovered, including pottery, fragments of boxes, copper tools, spindles for weaving, mats, sandals and children's toys. A number of papyri have also been discovered in the ruins. Apart from literary, medical, and mathematical texts, the documents included several property conveyances, lists of workmen, brick and construction accounts and temple archives. However, few give any details of the type of work performed in the construction of the royal buildings.

The use of the royal pyramid and its adjoining mortuary temple had one important drawback which invariably prevented the ruler from enjoying an eternal after-life surrounded by his treasures. The pyramid was much too conspicuous. When order broke down, the guard on the tomb was relaxed and the tomb-robbers came forward to loot the valuables. The danger of tomb-robbery was as old as the practice of stocking the tombs with valuable goods. Religious conservatism had no doubt prevented the royal architects from altering the hallowed formula of the pyramid. Change finally came in the early Eighteenth Dynasty from Thebes, where already in the Eleventh and Seventeenth Dynasties the shift to rock-cut tombs had begun. Now, in a major innovation, the tomb and mortuary temple were to be separated. The temple would be built on the edge of the desert and could be as conspicuous and imposing as the ruler's resources would allow, but the royal tomb would be hidden away in the inaccessible valleys of the western cliffs at Thebes and its pyramid top, a beacon to tomb-robbers, would be scrapped. However, the pyramid had for too long been associated with royal burial and the after-life to be discarded completely from funerary architecture. The abdication of this royal privilege meant that it now became free to be used by private individuals. Thus the private rock-cut tombs at Thebes soon sported a small pyramid atop the burial chamber.

The last ruler of Egypt to be buried in a pyramid-topped tomb (apart from the kings of the Twenty-fifth Dynasty who briefly revived royal pyramids) appears to have been Ahmose I, founder of the Eighteenth Dynasty (c. 1552 BC). Presumably some group of workmen must have been in existence to build his tomb, and those of his predecessors in the Seventeenth Dynasty, but no information is available about them. Ahmose I's son and successor, Amenhotpe I (c. 1527–1506 BC), was the first to build his tomb separately from his mortuary temple. He may have been the ruler who first formed the corps of workmen who were to become hereditary tomb-builders, but the only evidence to support this is that Amenhotpe I and his mother Ahmes-Nefertari were worshipped as patrons by the royal workmen in later times. However, the community certainly existed under his successor, Thutmose I (c. 1506–1493 BC). It

4 *Amenhotpe I (c. 1527–1506 BC); in a wall-painting from
a tomb of the Twentieth Dynasty, about four hundred years
after his death. He and his mother Ahmes-Nefertari were
particularly venerated, but other members of his immediate
family are sometimes depicted in Ramesside tombs.*

was during his reign that a wall of bricks stamped with the royal name was erected around a village in a small wadi, or valley, on the west bank of the Nile. The area is now called Deir el-Medina, and it is by this name that the village of the workmen also came to be known. Thutmose I also set another precedent: he chose to be buried in the hidden valley which is now known as the Valley of the Kings.

Very little documentation has survived from the earliest history of the community of Deir el-Medina. The select band of craftsmen were chosen to perform their work as speedily and as discreetly as possible. In later times the village came under the direct authority of the vizier, or prime minister, but it would appear that this was not the case in the Eighteenth Dynasty. The supervision of the construction of Thutmose I's tomb was delegated to Ineni, the overseer of construction at Karnak, the main temple to Amun on the east bank of the Nile. He had previously been involved in the erection of the two magnificent obelisks of Thutmose I at Karnak:

I supervised the excavation of the cliff-tomb of His Majesty alone, no one seeing, no one hearing . . . I was vigilant in seeking that which is excellent. I made fields of clay in order to plaster their tombs of the necropolis. It is a work such as the ancestors had not which I was obliged to do there.

Under Queen Hatshepsut (*c.* 1479–1458 BC) the construction of the royal tomb was supervised by Hapuseneb, the High Priest of Amun, although

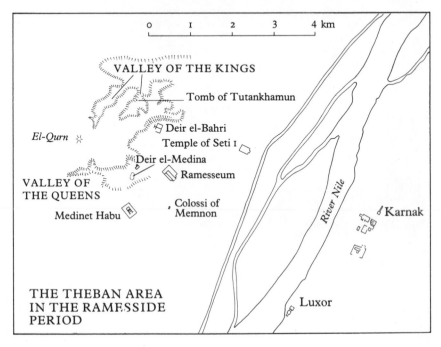

THE THEBAN AREA
IN THE RAMESSIDE
PERIOD

5 *Paintings from the tomb of Thutmose III (c. 1479–1425 BC). The tomb is
decorated in the plain painted style which was in use in the Eighteenth Dynasty and
which made the walls resemble a papyrus. In this view the king acts as a ferryman for
the goddess Isis (above); below (right) he is suckled by Isis in the form of a tree,
and (left) he is shown with his three queens and a daughter.*

it is not certain whether it was the tomb built for her as the queen of Thutmose II or, more probably, the royal tomb which she had built in the Valley of the Kings after her usurpation of the throne. A similar role was performed by the second prophet of Amun, Amenhotpe-si-se, for his sovereign Thutmose IV and by Maya, the overseer of the treasury, for his master Tutankhamun.

We know little of how the royal workmen of Deir el-Medina were organized at this period. They were called 'servants in the Great Place' and were under the direct control of one or more foremen known as 'overseers of construction of the Great Place'. They appear to have been segregated from the other groups of workmen on the west bank building the royal mortuary temples or excavating the tombs of the nobles. Some contemporary ostraca, inscribed potsherds or limestone chips, found in the area of Deir el-Bahri, give information about the work on the mortuary temples of Hatshepsut and Thutmose III. From these documents it would appear that the mass of workmen were conscripted in the time-honoured fashion to work on royal projects. They came from various regions, such as Esna and El-Kab to the south, or from royal and private estates. During this same period the architect Senenmut, who was in overall charge of the Deir el-Bahri construction, took the opportunity to build a private tomb for himself and his parents. Again, the labourers used for its excavation came from various places, as far afield as Hermopolis, Nefrusi and even Nubia. It would thus appear that private tomb-owners did not have the team of royal necropolis workmen at their disposal for this non-royal work. Certain masons and scribes are recorded as having worked on the tomb for several months. They probably came from a pool of skilled men available for use in the construction of private tombs but distinct from the royal workmen themselves.

The chief evidence from the site of Deir el-Medina in the Eighteenth Dynasty consists of the few tombs of this period that have been discovered in the valley which, with some pit-burials and a few stelae, are all that remain of the flourishing community of this time. The most important of the tombs is that of the foreman Kha, who appears to have died during the reign of Amenhotpe III (c. 1390–1352 BC). His chapel has been badly denuded and only a few fragments of wall-painting survive. However, his subterranean tomb has been discovered intact. The deceased lay in the innermost of two painted wooden coffins which rested in turn in a rectangular wooden sarcophagus covered by its original shroud. Garlands of flowers lay around the coffin. The sarcophagus and coffin of Kha's wife Meryt were nearby. Although she was buried in only one coffin, unlike her husband, her face was covered by a funerary mask of plastered linen which had been gilded and inset with glass eyes. The bodies, together with the rest of the contents of the tomb, were removed to the Turin Museum where they now rest. Recent x-ray studies have shown that Kha

6 *Painting from the tomb the workmen of Nu and Nakhtmin. This joint tomb is one of the few surviving from the Eighteenth Dynasty. The tomb-owners and their wives are shown offering to their respective parents.*

is adorned with ear-rings, a gold collar and bracelets, while his wife also wears a collar and ear-rings and a girdle composed of gold plaques and faience beads. The funerary equipment included a fine wooden statue of the deceased with its garland in place, alabaster and pottery vases, model vases, bronze vases, tools, *shabtis* in their box, furniture including two funerary beds and stools, ten assorted wooden boxes, a wig, a draughts-board, linen, and an especially fine papyrus.

In the reign of Akhenaten (*c.* 1352–1336 BC), the capital was moved from Thebes to Amarna. Much has been written about Akhenaten, his wife Nefertiti, and his religious reforms. In order to escape the influence of the Theban priesthood he built a new capital, Akhetaten, on a virgin site, now known as El-Amarna, on the east bank of the Nile in Middle

7, 8 *The tomb of the foreman Kha.*
Beyond the first doorway into the tomb
(which had been blocked with numerous
rough stones) lay a corridor in which
some grave goods had been deposited
(left). A second closed doorway at the
back of the corridor led into the main
burial chamber, part of which is
illustrated above, untouched since it
was closed. Kha and his wife were buried
in wooden sarcophagi, which are still
covered by their original shrouds.
9 (above right) *The inner and outer*
coffins of Kha, still decorated with their
original garlands.
10 (right) *The mummy of Kha. A*
recent X-ray has revealed an elaborate
collar and ear-rings. A girdle of Isis
amulet can be seen under the lower part
of the collar.

Egypt. In the cliffs on the same side of the river he ordered the excavation of a tomb for himself and his family:

There shall be made for me a tomb in the eastern mountain of Akhetaten. My burial shall be made there . . . and the burial of Queen Nefertiti shall be made there . . . and the burial of Princess Meritaten shall be made there . . . If I should die in any town of the north, south, west, or east . . . I shall be brought back and my burial made in Akhetaten. If Queen Nefertiti should die in any town of the north, south, west, or east . . . she shall be brought back and her burial made in Akhetaten. If Princess Meritaten should die in any town of the north, south, west, or east . . . she shall be brought back and her burial made in Akhetaten . . .

In a desert valley not far from his capital, a village was laid out by the royal architects for the workmen who were to build the royal tomb and probably the noble tombs at Akhetaten. The official role of the community

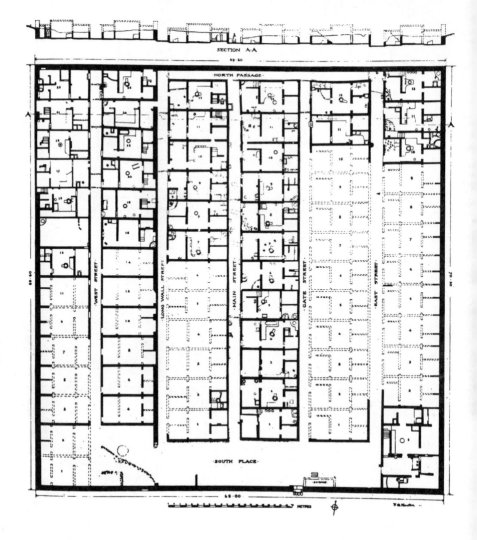

at Deir el-Medina presumably ceased when the Valley of the Kings was abandoned as a royal burial ground, although people probably continued to live on the site. It is not known whether any of the workmen were transferred to the new capital. In its completed state the village resembled a large square surrounded by mud-brick walls. Inside, five streets ran north and south to intersect with two streets which ran east to west at the north and south ends of the village although they did not run the full length of the town. Thus six large blocks each consisting of about twelve houses were formed. It appears that the two western blocks were built slightly later than the rest of the village and were originally separate from it. The village was entered by a gate in the south. A separate gate for the western section soon fell into disuse. The houses were built of mud-brick, but stone was used for some thresholds and wood for the door frames. The

11 (left) *A plan of the workmen's village at El-Amarna.*
12 (above) *The workmen's village at El-Amarna. The walls of the houses are still visible. El-Amarna was unusual in that the royal and noble tombs were located on the east bank of the Nile, instead of the west bank as was the normal practice.*

13　*The village of Deir el-Medina. In the foreground is the village, while behind on the slope of the cliff are the tombs of the workmen.*

flat roofs were made up of wood beams and matting. An average house comprised four rooms. The first was an entrance hall giving directly onto the street. It served as a storage area for cattle or as a work area. The second room was the main living quarters. It was higher than the previous room and had a wooden or stone column to support the roof. Small windows high up let in some light. There was a low brick platform or divan upon which the owner could sit or rest. This room would have been furnished with wooden stools as well as large water-storage jars. The third room served either as a store-room or bedroom, or both. The fourth room, at the side of the third, was the kitchen, which usually contained storage bins, an area for grinding wheat, an open hearth and an oven. The staircase to the roof could be in either the first, second or fourth rooms. These rooms were often decorated with frescoes or whitewash. A larger house near the entrance to the village was probably used by the chief foremen or police guard of the village. The Amarna village was abandoned together with the main city shortly after the death of Akhenaten.

In the reign of Tutankhamun (*c.* 1336–1327 BC) the royal court returned to Thebes, and the royal tomb was once more built in the Valley of the Kings. It is not clear whether Deir el-Medina once again became the headquarters of the royal workmen at this time. Certainly workmen were available to build the tombs of Tutankhamun and his successor Ay. However, an attempted robbery of the tomb of Tutankhamun shows that the area may not have been totally secure. The community at Deir el-Medina was certainly officially in operation by year 7 of Horemheb (*c.* 1317 BC) at the latest, since in that year certain tracts of land, including deserted tombs, were reassigned to members of the community by the chief steward of Thebes. We have little detailed information about the history of the site until the reign of Seti I (*c.* 1294–1279 BC) early in the Nineteenth Dynasty, by which time the community must have been well established. From the reigns of Ramesses II and his successors we have a wealth of evidence in the form of ostraca, papyri, stelae and tomb inscriptions. We know the names of the workmen and their wives and children; we can even pinpoint the houses of individual families, and from these sources we can build up a picture, in intimate detail, of the lives, and deaths, of the people of Deir el-Medina.

2 The Men of the Gang

THE FULL TITLE of a royal necropolis worker in the Eighteenth Dynasty was 'servant in the Great Place', or once, 'servant in the Beautiful Place of the mighty king'. In the Ramesside period they were called 'servants in the Place of Truth'. The workmen were known collectively as 'men of the gang' which was derived from the term for a ship's crew. Like an Egyptian ship's company, the gang was divided into two sides, right and left, although it is not certain that these sides actually worked the right and left sides of the royal tomb. The full complement of the gang seems to have varied. We know that in the middle of the reign of Ramesses II there were at least forty-eight men, but by the end of the reign the crew had been run down to about thirty-two. This probably indicates that the royal tomb had been completed and so less workmen were required. Those who remained were probably engaged in the construction of the tombs of minor members of the royal family. Presumably with the start of a new reign more men were enrolled to fill the gaps. In the reign of Ramesses III forty men are named, but in the reign of his successor Ramesses IV the gang was dramatically expanded to one hundred and twenty men. The new ruler obviously had grandiose plans to embark on a large-scale building programme in the necropolis, but in the event he only reigned six years. The numbers were then cut back to sixty. Deaths sometimes led to the two sides of the gang being out of equilibrium, but these were made up when the gaps were filled. Workmen were usually permanently attached to one side of the gang, but occasional transfers, temporary or permanent, are recorded. The work-force was largely recruited from the sons of workmen, but new recruits from outside the village were sometimes admitted. As the village families were large, there were always more applicants than places, so many younger sons had to leave the community to seek work elsewhere.

The work-force was controlled by two foremen, one for each side of the gang. The foreman was known as the 'overseer of construction in the Great Place' in the Eighteenth Dynasty and later more simply as 'chief of the gang in the Place of Truth'. Apart from the obvious purpose of keeping a tighter control on each side of the gang, having two foremen

14 Stela of the foreman Baki. The foreman and his son appear at
the top of this stela worshipping Ptah and Hathor. Below is a group
of contemporary workmen, including the village doctor Amenmose.

prevented a concentration of power in the hands of any one man in the village. Relations between the two foremen were not always smooth. The foreman Paneb once remarked to his colleague Hay: 'I will get you in the mountains and kill you'. Fortunately for Hay, Paneb did not carry out his threat. Whether the work ran smoothly must have depended largely on the respective characters of the foremen. They were theoretically appointed by Pharaoh himself, although in practice the decision appears to have been left to the vizier, who maintained direct control over the village and its activities. Bribery was not unknown, and at least one instance is recorded. It seems that the appointment was at first made on an individual basis, but in the Ramesside period it came to be regarded as the hereditary right of the holder's family. At the beginning of the Nineteenth Dynasty (c. 1295 BC) control of the left side of the gang was held by Pashed and Baki; these two men do not appear to have been related to each other, and it is not clear which of them held office first. The office of foreman was then acquired by Kaha, a son of a chief carpenter and possibly son-in-law of Baki. His family managed to hold on to the post of foreman with minor interruptions until the end of the Twentieth Dynasty.

The post of foreman on the right side was already hereditary in one family when our records begin. Neferhotep the elder held this position under Horemheb, Seti I and Ramesses II, and was succeeded by his son Nebnufer. He was in turn succeeded by his son Neferhotep the younger, who held office for the last half of the reign of Ramesses II, through the reign of Merenptah, and into the reign of Seti II. Neferhotep held the office for about forty or fifty years, so he must have been quite a young man when he first took over the job. His tomb was constructed towards the end of the reign of Ramesses II and is by far the largest and most splendid in the workmen's necropolis although now sadly ruined. Some ideal of the skilled craftsmanship which Neferhotep could call upon for his own use can be seen in a badly damaged votive stela which he commissioned.

Neferhotep was childless and seems to have brought up the son of one of his fellow workmen as a foster son, but the boy Paneb, already mentioned above, turned out to be a bad lot and is even accused of having threatened to kill Neferhotep:

Charge concerning his [Paneb's] running after the chief workman Neferhotep . . . although it was he who reared him. And he [Neferhotep] closed his doors before him, and he [Paneb] took a stone and broke his doors. And they caused men to watch over Neferhotep because he [Paneb] said: I will kill him in the night . . .

It seems that Paneb had a habit of making death threats to those who annoyed him. Neferhotep complained to the vizier about Paneb's behaviour and a suitable punishment was ordered to be meted out. However, Paneb was not without influence for he seems to have complained direct

16 (left) *Stela of Neferhotep. The figures of the deified king Amenhotpe I and his mother Ahmes-Nefertari are carved in raised relief in the upper register, while Neferhotep is shown in sunk relief in the lower register.*

15 (below) *The tomb of the foreman Neferhotep. This grandiose tomb has been badly damaged and little of its original internal decoration survives.*

17 Stela of Hesunebef.
The deceased foreman
Neferhotep is depicted at
the top of the stela. Below
Hesunebef, his family, two
other workmen and their
wives, and possibly
Neferhotep's widow, kneel
in adoration.

to Pharaoh himself about his treatment and the vizier who ordered it was himself dismissed.

Following his failure with Paneb, Neferhotep and his wife Webkhet turned their affection to a young male slave in their household named Hesunebef. In the innermost room of the chapel of Neferhotep's tomb the young boy is depicted at the side of his master's chair feeding a pet monkey. In the main hall of the chapel, which was presumably decorated later, the now adult Hesunebef is named as a workman. This change of status from slave boy to free royal workman was undoubtedly due to the influence of his master Neferhotep. Hesunebef even acquired a wife, Hunero, who was probably a local girl and possibly a relative of his former master. He named two of his children Neferhotep and Webkhet after his patrons and honoured the memory of Neferhotep with a votive stela. Unfortunately, his marriage was not a success and he divorced his wife towards the end of the Nineteenth Dynasty. Hesunebef was a member of the community into the reign of Ramesses III.

The foreman Neferhotep lived until his seventies but he was not destined to die in his bed. Amennakhte, his brother, reported that 'the enemy killed Neferhotep'. It is now certain that this phrase refers to a civil war which broke out in Egypt between the legitimate Pharaoh Seti II and a usurper, Amenmesse, who controlled Thebes for several years. Neferhotep seems to have been killed just before Thebes fell to the forces of Seti II. It is not known whether he was merely an accidental victim of the fighting or deliberately put to death by the usurper. Paneb seems to have taken advantage of the confusion and succeeded in being appointed Neferhotep's successor by handing over five of the late Neferhotep's slaves to the newly installed vizier of Seti II as a bribe. His criminal career as foreman will be dealt with in a further chapter, when justice at last seems to have triumphed. Following Paneb's removal, the position of foreman of the right was filled by the family of Nekhemmut, where it remained for most of the Twentieth Dynasty.

The 'scribe of the Tomb' was also appointed directly by the vizier. In the Nineteenth Dynasty there appears to have been only one official scribe although other less exalted scribes are known in the village, and they confusingly often style themselves scribes of the Tomb as well. Draughtsmen, and sometimes workmen, also call themselves scribes in some of their inscriptions and letters. Early in the Twentieth Dynasty the central administration seems to have recognized two official scribes, one for each side of the gang, and this system continued throughout the dynasty. The scribe's chief duty was to keep a register of work done and to note any absentee workers. He also recorded the removal of material from royal store-rooms and the payments of the workmen's wages.

The importance of the scribes and their vital role in the community are reflected in their many monuments at Deir el-Medina. A notable example is furnished by the scribe of the Tomb Ramose, who was appointed to this post in year 5 of Ramesses II (*c.* 1275 BC) and was still working in year 38 of the same reign. Previously he had been a scribe of the treasure of the funerary temple of King Thutmose IV and possibly a scribe of the funerary temple of Amenhotpe son of Hapu, a deified vizier of Amenhotpe III. Both of these temples were situated not far from Deir el-Medina on the western bank of the Nile. Ramose has left a large number of stelae and other monuments, including three tombs. Presumably he was buried in only one of them and, indeed, it appears that one of the others was used as the burial place of his female dependents. His wealth is also indicated by his ownership of slaves and farm land, and he is frequently depicted in the tombs of his fellow workmen. However, he suffered from the fact that he and his wife Mutemwia were childless. On two stelae he prayed to the deities of childbirth and fertility, and even dedicated a stone phallus to the fertility goddess Hathor with the inscriptions:

O Hathor, remember the man at his burial. Grant a duration in thy House as a rewarded one to the scribe Ramose. O Golden One, who lovest when thou desirest the praised one, thou desired one, cause me to receive a compensation of thy house as a rewarded one.

18 *Stela of the scribe Ramose. Ramose worships the god Ptah and the goddess of Truth, Maat.*

Unfortunately, Ramose had to be satisfied with an adopted son since his successor as scribe Kenherkhepeshef, son of Panakht, calls himself son of Ramose as well.

Kenherkhepeshef was probably a pupil and protégé of Ramose. His nearly illegible handwriting has been identified from several documents and has been found on an ostracon in the village dated to year 33 of Ramesses II (*c.* 1247 BC) when he was presumably still junior to Ramose. In year 40 he is named as scribe and there is no reason to doubt that he had succeeded as official scribe of the Tomb. He held office until the end of the reign of Seti II – a period of approximately forty-three years – and so was at least in his late sixties, if not older, when he disappears from view. He does not appear to have been a particularly conscientious or likeable person. There are two accusations of bribery against him and he is recorded as using men of the gang to do private work for him during official working hours. Indeed, he seems to have used his office to try to get them to do the work for free, since the draughtsman Parahotpe complained bitterly:

19 (above) *The dream-book of the scribe Kenherkhepeshef. The language of the text appears to date it to the Middle Kingdom, but this version was written down in the early Ramesside period prior to its acquisition by Kenherkhepeshef.*

20 (below) *The Battle of Kadesh. Part of the account of the 'victory' of Ramesses II over the Hittites has been copied by the scribe Kenherkhepeshef in his own hand on the back of the dream-book. Some ostraca in this same hand have been identified at Deir el-Medina. The full account of the battle of Kadesh is known from inscribed texts on the temples of Ramesses II and another papyrus.*

What does this bad way mean in which you behave to me? I am to you like the donkey. If there is some work, bring the donkey, and if there is some food, bring the ox. If there is some beer, you do not look for me, but, if there is work, you do look for me... I am a man who has no beer in his house. I try to fill my belly by my writing to you.

For all his faults, Kenherkhepeshef seems to have had some pretensions to learning, and by chance fragments of his private library have come down to us. The most interesting is a dream-book giving the interpretation of various dreams, the significance of which was readily apparent to ancient Egyptians, just as to modern psychiatrists. Among the various interpretations are:

If a man sees himself in a dream, looking out of a window; good, it means the hearing of his cry by his god.
If a man sees himself in a dream, sight-seeing in Busiris; good, it means having a great old age.
If a man sees himself in a dream, burying an old man; good, it means prosperity.
If a man sees himself in a dream, drinking warm beer; bad, it means suffering will come upon him.
If a man sees himself in a dream, seeing his face in a mirror; bad, it means another wife.

On the back of the dream-book, Kenherkhepeshef copied out in his own hand parts of the victory hymn of Ramesses II about the battle of Kadesh, where he claimed to have defeated the Hittite army. That claim is debatable, since the Hittite account which also survives ascribes the victory to its forces. Copies of this poem survive on the walls of the temples of Luxor, Karnak, Abu Simbel and Abydos, and the Ramesseum, but papyrus versions were also in circulation and doubtless the scribe was copying from one of these. The back also had a copy of one of his reports to the vizier on the progress of work on the royal tomb. His interest in history is shown by an ostracon in his hand and a stone altar both of which contain a list of royal names, some of them quite obscure.

There is one factor in the career of the scribe Kenherkhepeshef which is intriguing. His widow Naunakhte survived him by at least fifty-one years, during which time she remarried and had eight children by her second husband. When it is recalled that Kenherkhepeshef was in his late sixties at least when he disappears, Naunakhte was obviously the very young widow of a much older man. There is at present no evidence that Kenherkhepeshef had an earlier wife or children, although, as his tomb has never been found, relatively little is known of his private affairs. Much of his property went to his widow. The famous dream-book was eventually acquired by one of her sons by her second marriage. Naunakhte at any rate seems to have been fond enough of her elderly husband to name one of the sons of her second marriage after him.

In year 16 of Ramesses III (*c.* 1171 BC) Amennakhte son of Ipuy became scribe of the Tomb. He held this office until the reign of Ramesses VI

The Men of the Gang

(*c.* 1144–1136 BC), and during this time he played an active part in the affairs of the community. He appears to have been a draughtsman prior to his promotion and probably owed his appointment to the good offices of the vizier To, after whom he named one of his sons. Amennakhte managed in due course to pass his office on to his eldest son Harshire and it remained in this family for at least six generations. His descendants Dhutmose and Butehamun, who lived at the end of the Twentieth and the beginning of the Twenty-first Dynasty, played a prominent part in the later years of the village. The records of their private lives are somewhat confused, as it would seem from many of their letters which have survived that they suffered from an excess of wives. The wife of Dhutmose and mother of Butehamun was a lady Baketamun, but in his correspondence Dhutmose is very solicitous of the welfare of the lady Hemshire and her children. Similarly the known wife of Butehamun is the lady Akhtay, who certainly predeceased him, as his lament of her shows.

Oh thou noble chest of Osiris, songstress of Amun Akhtay who rests under thee. Listen to me and give the message. Tell her since thou art next to her: How do you fare? How are you? Thou shalt say to her: Woe Akhtay does not prosper so says your brother, your companion. Woe you beautiful one who has no equal. One does not find an example of any ugliness ... on you ... Good to me are my mother and father, brother and sister; they have come, but you have been taken from me.

In his letters, however, Butehamun appears to express affection for the lady Shedemde. Now, as most ordinary Egyptians usually had only one wife at a time, one could assume that father and son on becoming widowers both remarried. However, it seems that Baketamun and Akhtay are mentioned in the same letters as Shedemde and Hemshire, unless these are different people. Thus some mystery still remains as to the exact marital relationships of these two scribes.

The foremen and the scribe, or scribes, constituted the captains of the village. They were the liaison between the community and the higher authorities, notably the vizier and the overseer of the treasury. They oversaw the removal of material from the royal storehouses for use in the construction of the tomb, received and distributed the wages among the workmen, sat as the chief magistrates of the community on the local court and acted as chief witnesses for any oaths. Their duties also included recommending to the vizier candidates for vacancies in the work-force. This duty could prove rather lucrative as some were prepared to allow their choice to be swayed by bribery. The captains sometimes used their authority to make workmen carry out tasks for themselves, such as work on their tombs or on commissions, possibly without payment, and they could also use their position to accept commissions for work from outside the community, and naturally took the major part of the payment. They were certainly among the wealthier inhabitants of the village, but their

21 *Stela of Aapahte,
son of the foreman Paneb.
Aapahte is named as
deputy of the gang on this
stela; he is shown here in
adoration of the god Seth.*

families continued to live in the community and intermarry with the ordinary workers.

Each foreman was assisted in his duties by a deputy. It seems that the foreman usually named his eldest son, or some other relation, to this position if he was able. This was not always the case and we know of several deputies who bear no relation to the foreman under whom they served. However, in many cases the deputy could consider himself a future foreman whose tasks of supervision and distribution of supplies he was sometimes required to undertake. The deputy also served on the community court and witnessed oaths. The ration lists disclose that this position was in a sense honorific since the deputy received no higher wages than any of his fellow-workmen. A typical deputy was Anherkhau the younger son of the foreman Hay. Hay served from years 17 to 21 of Ramesses III (c. 1170–1167 BC), but in year 22 of that reign Anherkhau appears as foreman for the

22 *Painting from the tomb of the foreman Anherkhau, who is shown worshipping the benu-bird, better known in the classical world as the phoenix.*

first time. From this one can guess that Hay had recently died and Anherkhau had succeeded to his post. The office of deputy was then bestowed on the workman Hay, who appears to have been Anherkhau's foster-brother and son of the chief carpenter Amennakhte, but the post was eventually given to Anherkhau's son Kenna.

The 'guardians of the Tomb' were charged with the control of the royal storehouses, in which the tools and other materials necessary for construction were kept. These materials were handed over by the guardians only under the supervision of the foremen and scribe. There were either one or two guardians, and they were prominent members of the community, ranking in seniority after the captains. The guardian Penbuy left several beautiful monuments; on them, and in his tomb, he is named with different wives, so he seems to have been married at least twice. The post of 'door-keeper of the Tomb' seems usually to have been filled by two men, one for each side of the gang, but in the reign of Ramesses II there were three. Their function was to guard the entrance to the royal tomb and they appear to have worked in shifts so that one was always on duty. They also acted as bailiffs and debt-collectors for the community, and thus had a rather unsavoury reputation. Closely connected with the affairs of the community were the Medjay, or police, stationed somewhere on the west bank of the Nile to keep order and prevent unauthorized entry to the royal tombs. They were directly under the authority of the mayor of Thebes-West. The chief of police sat as a member of the community courts, and he and his men were involved in numerous commercial dealings with the royal workmen. There were probably two chiefs of police for the Deir el-Medina contingent.

The community was served by certain workers who were seconded to the village by the central administration. The 'servants of the Tomb' undertook the task of supplying certain provisions and doing specified tasks for the workmen. They consisted of wood-cutters, water-carriers, fishermen, gardeners, washermen and, at times, potters. They were under the direct control of the door-keepers and the scribes. These servants could rise to become fully-fledged workmen and, conversely, when the number of the work-force was reduced from 120 to 60, the 60 unemployed men were transformed into servants. The servants did not live in the village but probably down near the river, where the supplies which they brought the community were located. The workmen were also allocated the services of female slaves who belonged to the central government. These women were attached to the sides of the gang and their task was to grind into flour the grain supplied to the community by the authorities. Each family was allowed a certain number of days free service, but this right was not always taken up as it could be sold to other members of the community; for example, we read of 'the day when the mistress gave her day of servant to the workman Any'.

The staff of the work-force included stone-masons, carpenters and chief carpenters, sculptors and draughtsmen, each of whom specialized in different phases in the construction of the royal tomb. Their skills were passed on from father to son. The draughtsman Pay, who flourished under Ramesses II, had three sons who were also draughtsmen, as were some of their sons. The sculptor Piay had four sons, all of whom became sculptors, although one was also a carpenter. A part of the crew consisted of young men who were being trained as future workmen. Most of these were sons of workmen but some outside appointments were made. The community also consisted of the wives and children of the workers, and some of the young boys were used for occasional light work like carrying messages. They were known as 'children of the Tomb', although they were not officially part of the work-force. If they failed to find a place among the youths enrolled as workmen, they would be forced to leave the community and make their careers elsewhere. One of the younger sons of the foreman Neferhotep the elder became an army scribe of the 'lord of the two lands and officer of His Majesty', while another became 'first transport officer of His Majesty . . .' and door-keeper in the Ramesseum, which was not far away from his birthplace.

Of course, currency as such did not exist in ancient Egypt and the workmen were paid for their services in kind. The payments were authorized by the vizier and seem to have been paid through the royal treasury, although supplies were sometimes received from the storehouses of local temples. These supplies were destined for the work crew, its officers, the guardians, the door-keepers, and the female slaves. The chief payment consisted of monthly rations of emmer wheat, which would be ground into flour, and barley for making beer. Bread and beer were the two chief staples of the Egyptian diet. The surviving wage slips seem to indicate that the foremen and scribes received a somewhat higher salary than the ordinary workmen. The door-keepers, guardians and the workman who acted as the local physician also received higher payments but not as high as the captains. A certain category of workmen was paid less than their fellows, and it has been supposed that these were the young recruits who did not have a family to support, since the wages were meant to provide sustenance for the workmen and their families. Indeed, recent studies seem to suggest that these supplies were more than ample to cover the wants of each family, and the worker then possessed an excess which he could barter for other products. The female slaves were supplied with a much smaller ration, which presumably only covered their subsistence. Thus, if supplies were regularly maintained, the work-force would be receiving a real wage over and above the rate of subsistence.

Apart from the grain, the workmen were supplied by the central authorities with fish, vegetables and water, with wood for fuel and with pottery for household use. There were also more irregular deliveries of dates, cakes and ready-made beer. There was also a system of bonus payments which were issued on festival days or for special reasons. Apart from extra provisions of normal supplies, the bonus payments would include sesame oil, blocks of salt and natron, and, most important of all, meat – usually ox. The government also issued supplies of clothes, although not enough to clothe the entire community continuously. All these supplies which constituted the workmen's wages were divided up among the community by the foremen and the scribes. It should not be forgotten that the community also enjoyed free delivery of the goods by the servants of the Tomb and free work by the female slaves in the grinding of wheat into flour.

The delivery of supplies to the community was not, in fact, always regular and delays in payment would in due course cause hardship in the community, although the workers may have tended to exaggerate the effects. In year 29 of Ramesses III (*c.* 1158 BC) the supplies failed to arrive on time, so on the twenty-first day of the second month the scribe Amennakhte announced to the crew: 'Twenty days have elapsed in the month and rations have not been given to us'. On this occasion he went to the storehouse of the mortuary temple of King Horemheb, which was nearby, and obtained provisions for the gang. However, supplies continued to be delayed and in the sixth month the workmen went on strike and staged sit-down demonstrations before the funerary temples of Thutmose III, Ramesses II, and possibly Seti I:

It is because of hunger and because of thirst that we came here. There is no clothing, no ointment, no fish, no vegetables. Send to Pharaoh our good Lord about it and send to the vizier our superior, that sustenance may be made for us.

Following these disturbances, provisions were found for the work-force, but strikes erupted again later in the same year and in subsequent reigns. Under Ramesses XI the scribe Dhutmose had to journey south of Thebes to collect the grain from local temples and farmers for the community. He took along two door-keepers as protection against irate payers.

The government payments were not the sole source of income for the community. In modern terms a fair amount of moonlighting went on during rest days, and sometimes on company time. The task of the community was to prepare the royal tomb and sometimes the tombs of queens,

23 *Delivery ostracon, from the end of the Nineteenth Dynasty, recording the arrears of water due to certain workmen.*

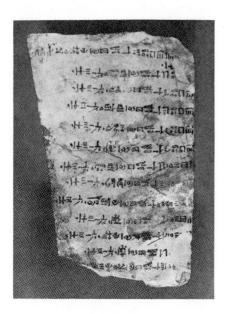

princes and honoured nobles. The tombs of the nobles on the west bank seem to have been constructed largely by other workmen hired for the task, although some may have come from the community. The workmen did not prepare the royal funerary equipment, which was fashioned in the royal workshops. In their spare time the workers built their own tombs in the mountain close to the community and made their own funerary equipment, including coffins, boxes and other items. The workers paid each other for various items of manufacture which they required, so there was a brisk trade in coffins and stelae. The scribes and draughtsmen who could paint the inscriptions in the necessary manner naturally charged the highest prices. Aside from doing work for the community, the workers also accepted outside commissions, either through the intermediary of the captains or directly, and so a certain amount of the tomb equipment used in private burials at Thebes was actually made at Deir el-Medina.

Frequent references to the possessions of the workmen show that they must have lived comfortably. Several workers owned their own expensive bronze tools, quite distinct from those provided by the government. Some workmen also owned cattle and donkeys, which could be let out at a profit if they were not being used by their owners. They often had real estate in the form of tombs and outhouses. The carpenter Ken left his son his mother's shares in the labour of several slaves. These shares do not appear to have been the same as the state servants, so perhaps several workmen or family members had clubbed together to buy slaves and share their labour. The foreman Neferhotep certainly had his own personal slaves. The scribe Ramose even owned land down by the cultivation which was farmed for him by his own servants, although he may have been a special case. The affluent status of the Deir el-Medina workmen was due in large measure to their privileged position as special state employees. In order to safeguard the right of the family to serve in this capacity, village officials are recorded on at least one occasion as receiving bribes to promote a workman's son: the father had apparently no difficulty in laying his hands on the necessary capital.

3 Building the Tombs

THE CHIEF TASK of the workmen of the village was to construct the king's tomb, where his body and possessions would rest until the end of time. During the Eighteenth Dynasty the Valley of the Kings came to be seen as the obligatory resting-place of the monarch, while the queens and princes were hidden away in the neighbouring valleys. Because of the importance attached to the royal burial place, one of the first acts of any reign was to order the immediate start of work on a new tomb. At Deir el-Medina the death of a ruler was greeted with jubilation, not sorrow, since work on the old tomb would be drawing to a close in the normal course of events. A new reign meant new work, quick initial payments and, often, bonus payments if the new king was in a hurry to provide for his eternal home:

On that day the vizier Neferrenpet came to the entrance of the Tomb and read them a letter saying that . . . Ramesses [VI] . . . had arisen as the great ruler of the whole land and they rejoiced exceedingly.

Some rulers, of course, sensed that time was not on their side and took extra precautions to ensure that their tomb would be near to completion when the time came for its use. Ramesses IV immediately increased the strength of the work crew from about 60 to 120. He certainly needed the extra men, since construction work did not begin on his tomb until his second year and he lasted only six full years. Yet his tomb was finished. Ay and Ramesses VI were more ruthless. They simply took over the unfinished tombs of their predecessors, whose remains were deposited in hastily built simple chambers. Such was the fate of the boy-king Tutankhamun; his successor Ay little dreamed that the sacrilege which he was committing by seizing his tomb would result in the protection of Tutankhamun and his treasures for millenia. Needless to say, Ay's tomb was thoroughly pillaged. From the viewpoint of the archaeologist and historian, the unfinished tombs are often more interesting than those which have been completed, since the process of construction is clearly visible there.

The first act in building a new tomb was to decide on a site in the Valley to begin excavations. The best sites would have been chosen by earlier

24 (above) *The Valley of the Kings. This view was taken towards the beginning of the century when the valley was less crowded with modern amenities and tourists.*

25 (left) *Ostracon recording the announcement to the workmen of Deir el-Medina of the accession of Ramesses VI (c. 1144 BC) to the throne of Egypt.*

kings and the cemetery was getting increasingly crowded by the end of the Ramesside period. It was, therefore, necessary to institute a careful probing of the Valley to discover a virgin site. In one case, during the construction of the tomb of Sethnakhte, the workmen broke into an adjoining tomb by mistake and the new tomb had to be abandoned. Sethnakhte remedied the situation by simply taking over the tomb of his predecessor. Several years later his son Ramesses III was faced with the prospect of having to abandon the tomb which had been begun for him because of the bad quality of the rock. He took over his father's original abandoned shaft and realigned the corridor so that it veered away from the adjoining tomb. The search for an appropriate site for the royal tomb appears to have been made under the watchful eyes of a royal commission headed by the vizier. When a suitable area was located, the commission could presumably sanction its use on the spot.

Next, a plan of the proposed tomb would be drawn up. It is not clear whether this was done solely by royal architects or by the senior members of the work crew. In either case, it would not have been difficult to conceive a plan, since it would usually follow the pattern set by its predecessors. The typical royal tomb was approached by means of a descending stairway set at an incline to the main doorway. Later Ramesside tombs usually had slides down the centre of the stairways to facilitate the entry of the royal sarcophagus into the tomb. From the entrance ran a series of halls and rooms of varying length and size, all built on a descending level. In the Eighteenth Dynasty the tomb contained a right-angled turn, but in the Ramesside period the tomb ran straight to the back. In the tombs of the Eighteenth and early Nineteenth Dynasties a pit was dug at the end of the front hall, cutting off access to the rest of the tomb except by a footbridge, which would have been removed when the tomb was completed. The doorway in the wall opposite the pit would have been sealed up and reliefs would have been painted over it so as to imply to potential tomb-robbers that the tomb ended at its first hall. Of course, no one was deceived by this manoeuvre. It has been argued that the pit had a cultic significance, but this seems less likely as its use was abandoned during the Nineteenth Dynasty. The pit also served, incidentally, to protect the tombs from flooding during the millenia in which they lay open and abandoned.

Towards the end of the tomb lay a broad pillared hall in which the sarcophagus rested. The more lavish tombs had a second pillared hall, or more, in the course of the tomb and numerous store-rooms leading off from the main burial chamber. Thus, although all the tombs were built to the same general plan, slight variations gave each some degree of individuality. Any major innovations were due to unforeseen circumstances, and extra time and resources becoming available. Of course, a plan of the proposed tomb would be available for the workmen to consult,

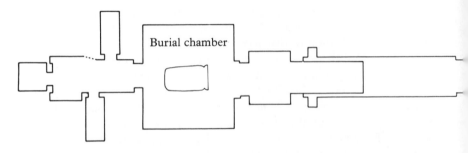

Burial chamber

26 (above) *A modern plan of the tomb of Ramesses IV.*
27 (below) *A plan on papyrus of the tomb of Ramesses IV. Unfortunately the plan is not complete, but can be compared with the modern plan of the same tomb.*

and by chance two have survived from ancient times. A plan of the tomb of Ramesses IX, painted on stone, was actually found abandoned in the very tomb itself. A second plan, which is incomplete, is written on papyrus and depicts part of the tomb of Ramesses IV.

Once the site had been chosen and the plan had been drawn up, the workmen began to cut the tomb out of the solid rock. The quarrying was done with a copper or bronze spike which would split the stone when pounded by a heavy wooden mallet. The workmen could also use a heavy wooden-handled bronze hoe, which would have been wielded like a modern pick-axe. These tools were the property of the state and would be handed out to the workmen when they were required. The scribe of the Tomb would carefully record who was given what and would expect the tools to be returned when they were no longer needed or when they had become blunt and had to be repaired and resharpened. They would then be put back in the government storehouse for future use. A workman might possess his own private tools, but he would not have used these on government work when freely available state tools were on offer. Most of the chippings formed by the excavations would be removed by leather or wicker baskets and scattered on the floor of the valley, although, in the

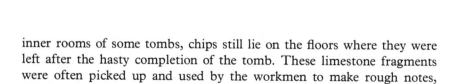

inner rooms of some tombs, chips still lie on the floors where they were left after the hasty completion of the tomb. These limestone fragments were often picked up and used by the workmen to make rough notes, designs, or even permanent records, and are known as ostraca.

As the stone-masons cut away the halls of the tomb, the plasterers were hard at work behind them on the walls. The uneven surfaces were covered with a layer of gypsum and whitewash to make them as smooth as possible. The method of supplying the workers with gypsum seems to have varied from period to period. At one time specific gypsum-makers were attached to each side of the gang to burn the raw gypsum and mix it with water to form the plaster. At other times this task was performed by specifically designated workmen, who would necessarily be excused from work in the Valley while they were busy at this task. The finished walls would then be turned over to the attention of the draughtsmen.

28 *Ostracon of a workman. The workman is depicted in action, breaking up the stone with his spike and mallet.*

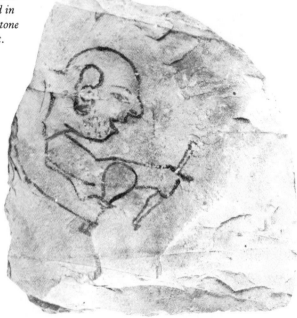

Building the Tombs

The scenes and reliefs which appear on the walls of the royal tombs consist solely of religious texts which mark the journey of the sun-god Re, with whom the dead king was identified, through the underworld in the evening. This journey would end in the room in which the royal sarcophagus was situated. From here the king-sun-god would be expected to rise each morning to begin his journey through the heavens before returning to the underworld in the evening. The texts in the tombs are all similar and were presumably copied from standard reference works. There are no historical texts and definitely no curses in any of the tombs. The draughtsmen would first set out the proposed texts and designs on the plastered walls in red ink. The master draughtsman would then correct these in black ink to ensure that the design and wording was perfect. This was contrary to the general practice elsewhere of using black ink for the first draft and red ink for the corrections.

In the Ramesside period the wall would next be turned over to the sculptors, who would carefully carve out the texts and designs with a wooden-handled bronze chisel. The type of relief used in the royal tombs

29 *The tomb of Seti I. The outline sketches on the walls in this part of the tomb have been completed, but no carving of the reliefs had yet begun. Work was presumably stopped on the death of the King.*

30 (above) *The tomb of Horemheb. The reliefs have been sketched and corrected, but only part of the lower scene has been carved.*

31 (right) *The tomb of Seti I. The carving of the reliefs in this part of the tomb has been completed, but the painting has not been finished. The King is shown in the presence of the goddess Isis, on the left, and the god Anubis, on the right.*

49

is known as raised relief, as the finished design is higher than the surface around it. This effect is produced by cutting away the surface surrounding the figures. The other form of relief, known as sunk or incised relief, produces designs which are cut below the surface and was usually used on temple walls. The final phase in preparing the walls of the royal tomb would be to paint the reliefs and inscriptions. Early tombs of the Eighteenth Dynasty were all painted without any carved reliefs. The ceilings of the tombs were usually just painted to represent the sky with stars or astronomical scenes. The paints were all made from a mineral base. Carbon would be used to produce black, ochre or iron oxide for red, calcium carbonate or sulphate for white, yellow ochre for yellow, azurite for blue and malachite for green. Various minerals could be combined to give various shades of colour. All the phases of construction – excavation, plastering, designing, carving and painting – would be going on at once in different rooms of the tomb. When the royal sepulchre was nearing completion, the great stone sarcophagus, which would have been prepared in a royal workshop and not by the workmen of Deir el-Medina, would be manoeuvred into position in the burial chamber.

Naturally, as the work progressed deeper and deeper, the natural sunlight which might illuminate the first rooms would fade, and it would be necessary to provide artificial lighting. The workmen were supplied with wicks made up of twisted pieces of linen which had been greased with oil or fat. Sesame oil is known to have been one of the lubricants which was used. Salt would have been employed to prevent the wicks from smoking and damaging the tomb. It seems likely that these wicks or candles were stood in pottery bowls which might have contained more than one wick. Careful accounts were kept of the number of wicks issued from the royal storehouse and consumed in the course of the work each day. There are also references to the fact that some of these wicks were made in the village by the workmen, who were issued with old clothes and linen for this purpose and expected to return the equivalent of completed wicks to the authorities.

The preparation of the royal tomb could be interrupted at any time by the death of the reigning pharaoh. In such a case the detailed decoration would be suspended in favour of feverish attempts to make the tomb presentable for the royal burial. This would normally take place within three months of the death after the seventy-day period of mummification. The royal regalia and funerary equipment, which would have been manufactured in the royal workshops in the course of the reign, would now be shipped to Thebes, if they had not already been stockpiled in the vicinity in readiness for their eventual use. Some of the items may not have been made especially for the burial: some pieces in the tomb of Tutankhamun were royal heirlooms or property from the previous reign which had been taken out of store for the occasion. We have no detailed explanation of

32 *The main burial chamber of the tomb of Seti I. The royal sarcophagus was removed to London by Belzoni at the beginning of the nineteenth century.*

the procedures which were involved in a royal funeral. Part of the proceedings included the Opening of the Mouth ritual, whereby the new king would symbolically revivify the mummy of his predecessor. Indeed, it was generally considered that the new king could not have legitimately ascended the throne without first performing the burial rites of his predecessor.

In the course of about four hundred and twenty years, approximately sixty-two tombs were built in the Valley of the Kings, and there are indications that several more may have been begun. Twenty-three grand royal tombs represent a sequence of twenty-five kings and queens-regnant of the Eighteenth to Twentieth Dynasties, as Sethnakhte usurped the tomb of Tewosret, and Ramesses vi that of Ramesses v. Tutankhamun and Smenkhkare, were buried in simple tombs of only a few rooms. There are also the beginnings of the first tombs of Ramesses ii and Ramesses iii, which were abandoned as unsafe. Three uninscribed tombs were probably meant for royal owners. The remaining tombs in the Valley consist of small and often undecorated corridor or pit-tombs which were built for junior members of the royal family or courtiers whom the king wished to honour, such as Yuya, father-in-law of Amenhotpe iii. One tomb of the Nineteenth Dynasty belonged to the all-powerful chancellor Bay, whose influence was paramount in the reign of the young Siptah. Most of these small tombs remain anonymous. Five tombs in the Valley have been found more or less intact. Three are readily identifiable – those of Yuya, Tutankhamun and Mahirper, fan-bearer of the time of Hatshepsut – although the last two had been partially robbed at one time. Two other uninscribed tombs (Tombs 55 and 56) had been badly damaged by water but were also untouched. Tomb 55 dated from the period immediately after Akhenaten and contained a body now identified as Smenkhkare. Tomb 56 was filled with jewellery from the time of Seti ii and may have been intended for one of his children. Several of the robbed tombs still had a small number of minor objects, such as, among others, funerary statues from the tomb of Ramesses i, vases from that of Merenptah, *shabtis* from that of Seti i, and funerary deposits from that of Ramesses xi. The tomb of Amenhotpe ii was later to be used to store several of the royal mummies which had been rescued from their pillaged tombs in the Twenty-first Dynasty. The Valley and its tombs have never been completely and accurately published. It is hoped that this work may be accomplished in the next few years.

The workmen did not of course work every day. The working week seemingly consisted of eight days, with rest days on the ninth and tenth. As the Egyptian month was composed of thirty days, this meant in theory six days of rest per month, although the workers seem to have taken long or three-day weekends quite frequently. Other free periods were sometimes available during the working week as well, so the workmen were obviously not pushed too strenuously. Additionally there were holidays on the religious festivals of the major gods of the community and Thebes, some of which could last several days. The working day apparently consisted of two shifts of about four hours each, with a break about noon for lunch. Sometimes it appears that the gang took the afternoon off as well. While at work in the valley, the crew would camp overnight in the vicinity. In fact, the remains of buildings, which have been excavated on the pass leading from Deir el-Medina Valley to the East Valley of the Kings, have been identified as the workmen's huts. The comfortable seat of the scribe Kenherkhepeshef was found here, with his name inscribed on it to prevent any other worker from using it.

The scribe of the Tomb was charged with keeping the attendance register of the workmen. The surviving examples show clearly that then as now workers could be absent from their jobs for a variety of reasons. A workman might be absent on the orders of his superior to do personal work for him, such as making his tomb equipment or tending his cattle, although such actions might not be considered strictly proper. Personal illness also accounted for a fair number of absences. The illness of one workman often entailed the absence of one or more of the others to nurse him. In year 40 of Ramessess II (c. 1240 BC) Paherpedjet, who must have functioned as the village doctor at that time, was away tending the ailing Aapahte in the third month of Akhet and the following month. He was

33 *The workmen's huts near the Valley of the Kings. These served as temporary resting places during the week so that the workmen did not have to return to the village each night.*

34 *Limestone attendance register. The name of each workman, and days on which he was absent, are carefully noted. Reasons for absence are indicated in red above each recorded non-attendance.*

later busy tending the workman Khons, the wife of the scribe, and the workman Haremwia. He does not appear to have been able to do much ordinary work. The only causes of illness specifically mentioned are scorpion bites and eye diseases. Family events might also prevent a workman from turning up in the valley, as some obscure excuses might refer to purification rituals after childbirth. A death in the family was an even more compelling reason. In year 40 of Ramesses II Neferabu was away embalming his brother, while Hehnekhu was busy bandaging the body of his mother. In another case, a workman was absent mummifying one of his colleagues. Personal religious reasons were often a cause for absences, as workmen would be away making offerings to the gods, possibly on recovery from illness. A workman would also be away on his 'festival'; this may not mean his birthday, since a festival celebrated by Khons lasted two days. Workmen could be away brewing beer, possibly for religious festivals. There were also less pleasant family occurrences, such as a row with the wife, which resulted in time off. Finally, there were reasons which do not seem as if they should have been regarded with much justification by the higher authorities: Pendua was away for a day drinking with Khons, while Wadjmose took a day off to build his house.

During a long reign such as that of Ramesses II or Ramesses III the workmen would have managed to finish the royal tomb long before the death of the monarch. If they had not already been ordered to do so, their talents could now be used for the benefit of other members of the royal family. Very little information has survived on the construction of these tombs. It is certain that the craftsmen were employed to build the highly decorated tombs of the royal wives and princes in the Valley of the Queens, such as the famous tomb of Queen Nefertari, wife of Ramesses II. These

54

35 *The tomb of Queen Nefertari. This splendidly painted tomb of the favourite wife of Ramesses II, situated in the Valley of the Queens, was doubtlessly constructed by the royal workmen of Deir el-Medina.*

were less elaborate constructions than the kings' tombs and consequently took less time to build. It may be that the workmen were occasionally allowed to work on the tomb of a noble, but it appears that usually the nobles, like Senenmut in the Eighteenth Dynasty, had to find their own builders. That would not necessarily be difficult as the community produced an excess of craftsmen who would no doubt find work from private patrons. The workmen themselves also enjoyed a regular and profitable supplement to their wages by making funerary equipment for private individuals – coffins, stelae, amulets, and other paraphernalia.

Apart from their work on the tomb of their royal master and the production of funerary equipment for private customers, the workmen were also busily engaged, when time allowed, in the construction of their own tombs. These were built into the cliff face just to the west of the village or on the lower slopes of these cliffs. Each had its individual variations, but basically all seem to have been built to a standard design. A small courtyard was laid out around the face of the cliff and separated from the

55

36 (above) *The tombs of the workmen on the slope of the cliff by the village.*
37 (below) *A typical Deir el-Medina tomb. This drawing shows the open courtyard and the vaulted chapel surmounted by a brick pyramid with a pyramidion. A shaft in the courtyard leads to an underground passage and the vaulted burial chamber.*

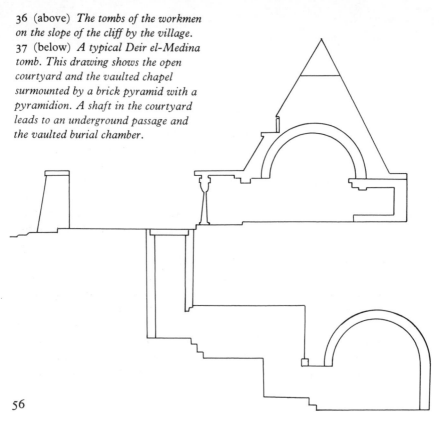

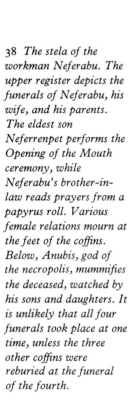

38 *The stela of the workman Neferabu. The upper register depicts the funerals of Neferabu, his wife, and his parents. The eldest son Neferrenpet performs the Opening of the Mouth ceremony, while Neferabu's brother-in-law reads prayers from a papyrus roll. Various female relations mourn at the feet of the coffins. Below, Anubis, god of the necropolis, mummifies the deceased, watched by his sons and daughters. It is unlikely that all four funerals took place at one time, unless the three other coffins were reburied at the funeral of the fourth.*

courtyards of neighbouring tombs by mud-brick walls. A small chapel was then cut out of the rock, or built of mud-brick if it was located on the lower levels. This chapel might consist of only a single room for an ordinary workman, but in the case of a foreman there might be a hall leading to a chapel and a shrine behind it. The ceiling of the chapel might be flat, but it could also be vaulted. A small pyramid, once the symbol of royalty, but now in common use for private burials, was erected above the roof of the chapel. Built of mud-brick, the pyramid would have stelae fixed on the sides and would be topped with a small stone pyramidion, also decorated on all four sides. The pyramidion and stelae would be dedicated to the sun-god Re-Harakhty. In the courtyard of the tomb a stela, about the size of a man, might be erected in memory of the deceased depicting in detail the burial ceremonies.

Building the Tombs

The shaft which led to the underground burial chamber was located either in the chapel or, more usually, in the courtyard. The fact that their shafts were not in their chapels but outside and difficult to locate helped to protect tombs such as these of Kha and Sennedjem from robbery. The underground burial chamber usually consisted of a large vaulted room, although there were sometimes other rooms with flat ceilings. Both the burial chamber and the chapel were brightly painted with lively scenes. These included religious texts and scenes of the gods and the underworld,

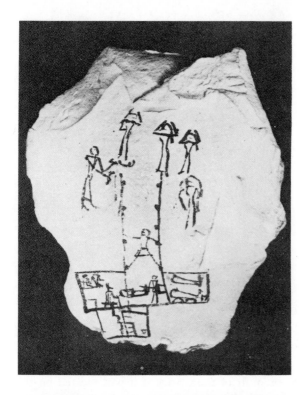

39 (left) *A burial. This drawing on an ostracon, possibly from Deir el-Medina, depicts the lowering of a coffin down the burial shaft to join other coffins in a family tomb. One of the attendants appears to wear an Anubis mask, although this depiction might be symbolic. At the top of the shaft the women mourn.*

40 (below) *Fragment of a stela of Neferabu. The relief shows the sons and relations of the deceased carrying assorted funerary goods to place in his tomb. These include various boxes and stools.*

as well as scenes showing the deceased with his family and his neighbours. There were even scenes which showed the funeral of the deceased. The burial chamber would house the coffins of the owner, his wife, and possibly other members of the family and all the goods which they wished to bring with them to the hereafter. Following the funeral, the burial chamber would be sealed with a wooden door; the door to Sennedjem's burial chamber has been found intact. Of course, not all members of the community had the time and the resources to prepare such elaborate tombs,

41 *Painting from the tomb of the workman Sennedjem.*
Sennedjem and his wife are receiving a libation from their
son Bunakhtef. Under their chairs their youngest children
are shown with side-locks of hair, to indicate youth.

and many smaller pit-tombs have been found outside the walls of the village.

It is most unlikely that any workman could have constructed an elaborate tomb on his own and so he must have had the help of his family and neighbours, either in return for payment or for like services. The records show that the foremen and scribes would make use of their authority to employ the work-force to build their tombs. The use of painted scenes, rather than painted relief as in the royal tombs, obviously helped to cut down the amount of work required. Equipment for the tomb, such as coffins, was made in the village by the workmen themselves. A craftsman would then pay one of the draughtsmen or scribes to add the necessary inscriptions:

What the draughtsman Neferhotep gave to Haremwia:
one wooden stela of Nefertari, while he gave to me one chest in exchange for it.
Also I decorated two coffins for him . . . and he made one bed for me.

Two coffins were usually required for each individual burial. The inner coffin showed the deceased in normal daily attire, while the outer coffin depicted him as a mummy. The face of the actual mummy would be covered with a cartonnage funerary mask. This was made from compressed linen covered with a thin layer of plaster and then painted. The coffins would be placed one inside the other and then put in a large wooden sarcophagus in the tomb. The funerary equipment would also include the four canopic jars in which the soft materials removed from the body in the course of mummification would be stored. These jars were placed in a large canopic chest. Other essential items for the burial were *shabtis*, or servant figures, in the *shabti*-box and a funerary papyrus which contained prayers for the deceased. Additional funerary objects might include small shrines and wooden funerary statuettes. Apart from these purely funerary objects, the tomb-owner would take some of his wordly goods with him as well – furniture, clothing, jewellery, tools, and pottery and stone vessels. In some cases models of expensive vases were provided. The workman Sennedjem even took his measuring equipment. The work on the tomb and the preparation of its equipment went on steadily during the life of the owner. The funeral scenes in the tombs were not of the actual event, but were idealistic and thus the owner might choose who would appear at his own funeral. The large funerary stelae in the courtyards of the tombs were composite depictions of the funerary rites of the owner, his wife and parents which obviously did not all take place at the same time. After death, it appears, the members of the community were embalmed in the village by their relatives and friends and not by special embalmers. It is also likely that the funerals were conducted by the workmen themselves acting as priests.

The bulk of the highly decorated and elaborate tombs date to the

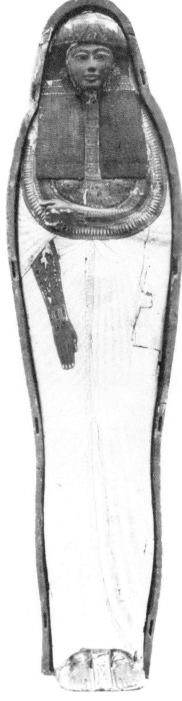

42 The inner and outer coffins of Iineferti, wife of Sennedjem.
The outer coffin depicts the mummiform figure, while the inner coffin
shows the lady as she might have been arrayed in daily life.

43 Shabti-*box of Nakhtamun. This box would have been filled
with* shabtis, *or servant figures, who would be destined to do any
work that the deceased was required to perform in the next life.*

44 Book of the Dead *of the foreman Pashed. The large fragment of a papyrus contains a prayer to the sun-god Re, who is shown as a falcon perched on the standard of the West. He is worshipped by Isis, Nephthys, and four baboons.*

45 *The Tomb of Kha. A fine wooden funerary statue from the tomb of Kha stands on a chair next to a* shabti *figure.*

Building the Tombs

reign of Ramesses II (*c.* 1279–1212 BC). A few earlier burials, such as that of Kha and Sennufer, have been found. It appears that on the reorganization of the village about year 7 of Horemheb (*c.* 1317 BC) older tombs were reassigned, while new ones were built. These tombs were not used just once, as they were originally designed to hold both the owner and his wife, who normally must have died at different times. Moreover, later descendants did own and use these tombs. In the tomb of Sennedjem his wife, son, daughter-in-law and other relations were buried with him. In the tomb of his son Khabekhnet are inscriptions of descendants of the family in the Twentieth Dynasty. These tombs were considered valuable pieces of real estate and passed by will down the family. Sometimes, of course, the location or ownership of a tomb might be lost. In year 25 of Ramessess III (*c.* 1162 BC) a ruined tomb was discovered. A special commission of workmen made an inventory of its contents before solemnly sealing it up again. There were also disputes regarding the ownership of tombs. In one case, a claimant rudely ejected the mummy of a member of his rival's family from the contested tomb. It seems that conditions in the Twentieth Dynasty were less propitious for elaborate tomb-building, although there are a few tombs which date to this period. Others, known to have existed from local records, can no longer be located. The scribe Amennakhte, who lived under Ramessess III and some of the succeeding reigns, built a tomb for himself that his great-grandson used to store documents. It is now unidentifiable.

The tombs of the workmen are an invaluable source of information about the people of Deir el-Medina. The workmen are portrayed in paintings with their families or their colleagues. Sadly, many of these tombs have met the same fate as the royal burials and have been plundered of the goods locked inside them. Presumably the bulk of the robberies must have occurred only after the village was abandoned, for it is unlikely that the members of the community would openly and systematically pillage the tombs of their own dead.

4 Village Life at Deir el-Medina

THE VALLEY OF Deir el-Medina, situated in the cliffs opposite Thebes, was an ideal location for the establishment of a community dedicated to a very discreet royal enterprise. The village was hidden from the river and could only be approached along a narrow road which ran north – south through the valley. It lay close to the Valleys of the Kings and Queens, where the work of the men would be concentrated. However, the valley and its inhabitants were not totally cut off from the outside world, as servants bringing supplies were constantly journeying up from the river and the workmen and their families would no doubt venture down to the cultivation from time to time to buy goods, transact business, and look after their land and other property which they owned outside the village proper.

The earliest village appears to have been laid out in the reign of Thutmose I (c. 1506–1493 BC), whose name is stamped on the mud-bricks of the wall that surrounded the first community. The wall seems to have been 6 to 7 metres in height and 105 centimetres thick. We have little evidence about the village in the Eighteenth Dynasty. It seems that it did not take up the entire area behind the wall, but that there was some open space for village animals, such as cattle. The first village was destroyed by fire, possibly during the Amarna period when it may have been temporarily abandoned. During the reign of Horemheb (c. 1323–1295 BC) the village seems to have been reorganized. The older houses were refurbished and new ones were built. The village expanded to the south and west and spilled out over the wall of Thutmose I. A new stone wall was built to enclose the suburbs. Still the village grew and new quarters sprang up outside the enlarged wall. At its height, probably in the reign of Ramesses II, the village comprised an area of about 132 metres long by about 50 metres wide. It contained seventy houses, while another forty or fifty lay outside the wall. The original village was bisected by one main street which ran from north to south, but a few side alleys were created when the village was expanded. These lanes were extremely narrow and may indeed have been covered over. Outside the north gate of the village lay the community well, which was filled by water-carriers from the Nile. Individual water-storage jars stood in front of the private dwellings.

Map of the village of Deir el-Medina and environs including the great pit and the tombs where the Saite sarcophagi were found. The many pit tombs around the village are noted.

Cemeteries

Cemeteries

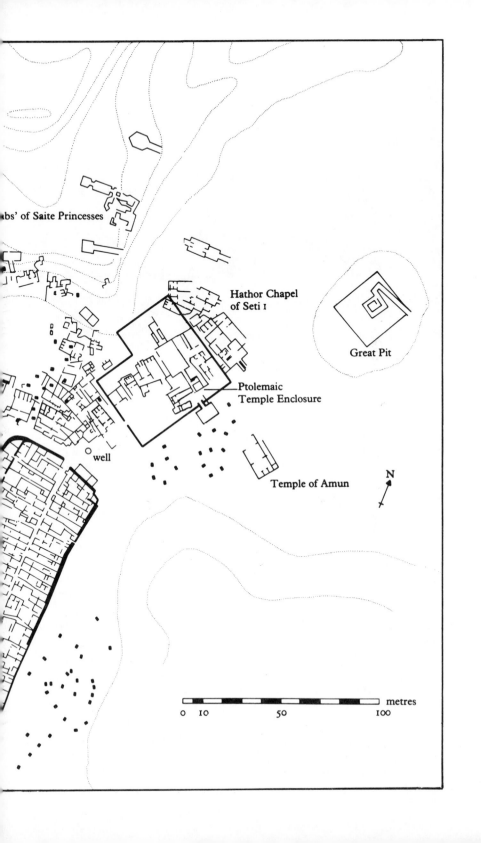

bs' of Saite Princesses

Hathor Chapel
of Seti I

Great Pit

Ptolemaic
Temple Enclosure

well

Temple of Amun

N

metres
0   10   50   100

46 *The village of Deir el-Medina. One of the main streets is clearly visible.*

The houses in the village opened directly on to the main street. They appear to have been assigned to the original inhabitants by the government, but then were treated as hereditary tenancies by the families who occupied them. The original houses, built on virgin soil, had no foundations and were composed of mud-brick. Later houses built on rubble or less favoured ground had basements of stone or brick and stone walls up to 2.5 metres in height topped by mud-brick. The houses varied from 3 to 5 metres in height and appear to have consisted of only one storey. The roofs were invariably flat and made up of tree trunks and palm leaves with spaces filled by pottery fragments and then plastered. The whole was 10 to 20 centimetres thick. The roof served as a protection during the heat of the day and as a terrace during the cool of the evening. There were some small holes left in the roof at selected places to let in light to the rooms below. As it seldom rained in this part of the country, no problems from weather were expected apart from an occasional dust storm.

The design of the houses followed a similar pattern throughout the village, with variations due to the social status and wealth of the owners. The house was painted white on the outside, apart from the wooden door which was red. The door jambs and lintels often bear texts which enable the owners of some houses to be identified; they were made of stone or wood and the hieroglyphs were painted red. The threshold could be either wood or stone. The floors were composed of hard-packed earth.

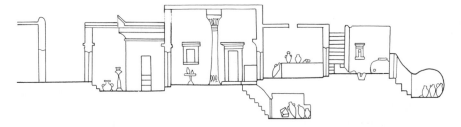

47 *A typical Deir el-Medina house. The house consisted of three main rooms and a back yard where cooking was carried out.*

In the grander residences the floors and walls might be plastered and painted white or red. An average house consisted of four rooms. The first room was entered directly from the street and was 40 to 50 centimetres below the level of the street. The chief feature of the entrance hall was a large brick structure in one of the corners of the room. It was generally rectangular in shape and measured 170 by 80 centimetres and was 75 centimetres high. It was approached by a flight of three to five stairs. The block was surmounted by a brick superstructure reaching almost to the ceiling so that it resembled a canopied four-poster bed in brick. The exterior of the block could be plain or decorated with frescoes. The most common decoration which survives depicts the god Bes, a familiar deity associated with childbirth, although other fragments show female figures. It has been assumed that the brick 'bed' was used by the women of the household for bearing their children, and was thus venerated as the link between the ancestors of the home-owner and future generations. However, it is conceivable that the brick structure was only an altar and not necessarily a birthing bed. This first room also contained niches for offering-tables, stelae or ancestral busts. It was probably an informal household chapel for the inhabitants, their ancestors and descendants.

The second room was loftier than the first and its roof was supported by one or more columns, made of limestone or the trunk of a palm tree, plastered over and set on a stone plinth. The main feature of this room was a low platform or divan of mud-brick about 20 centimetres off the ground with higher projecting sides at each end, sometimes made of stone. The top of the platform was plastered and whitewashed. It doubtless served as a seating area by day and a bed by night. The room also contained a false-door stela dedicated to a favoured deity. There might be yet more niches for shrines or stelae. Underneath the divan a small cellar might be located where household goods might be stored. In a few houses child burials have been discovered beneath this main living-room. The room itself was lit by windows set high up in the walls. Off this main room were one or two small rooms which appear to have been used as store-rooms, work areas and sleeping quarters for the female members of the household. At the back of the house was a walled open area which served as the kitchen, where flour was prepared by grinding the grain supplied by the central authorities. A small oven of brick or pottery was located there to bake the all-important bread. The excess grain might be stored in a silo also placed in this rear courtyard, and there might also be another cellar here for the storage of pottery. A stairway from this back court led up to the roof. The whole house was sparsely furnished with only a few stools and tables and, of course, the standard head-rest, used by the Egyptians in the place of pillows. Most of the household items not in constant use would be stored away in jars or baskets.

The life of the village was presumably carried on during the week by the women, while their menfolk worked away at the royal tombs. Of course, there were always some men about – retired workers, invalids, men on special duty in the village, men excused work and servants bringing up goods from the river. The prime duty of the wife of a workman would be to look after his home. Unlike the wives of ordinary workers, her work load would have been lightened by the government provision of

48 *The ruins of a house at Deir el-Medina. Part of a column and the base of another can be seen in the foreground.*

49 *Limestone head-rest of the scribe Kenherkhepeshef, with fabulous creatures and inscribed with prayers. Head-rests were used by the Egyptians instead of pillows, but this one was destined for the tomb and not intended for domestic use.*

female slaves to grind her corn, though if the lady of the house chose to sell these services, she would naturally be obliged to do the work herself. She would also be responsible for the preparation of the staple diet of bread. Her duties would include the provision of clothing for the family, since the government supply was inadequate, and might pass some of her day weaving and sewing. One of the accusations made against the foreman Paneb was that he forced the wives of workmen to weave clothes for himself, presumably without charge, but a clever seamstress could not only clothe her family but might also bring in a tidy income for herself. The wife also had to tend the young children, which was not a simple task, as at Deir el-Medina families were large, often numbering as many as fifteen. Of course, many children must have died in childhood. Like most ordinary Egyptians, a workman would have only one wife at a time, but death or divorce could set him free to remarry. It is unlikely that any but elderly adults remained single for long, as marriage was regarded as the normal state in the ancient world.

The important role of the wife and mother was recognized by her place in Egyptian society. The wife was an equal with her husband under Egyptian law. She was left in full control of her own property, acquired by inheritance, both before and after marriage. She also acquired the right to a third of the marital property, although it is not clear if this covered the husband's personal property before marriage or only property acquired after marriage. This right remained only theoretical while the marriage endured, but on the death of the husband the third reverted to his wife, while the rest of his property went to his heirs, one of whom might, of course, also be his wife. If the wife died before the husband, the third did not revert to him, but the right to it remained vested in her heirs. The lady Naunakhte, who had already inherited from her first childless marriage, specifically disinherited several of the children of her second

71

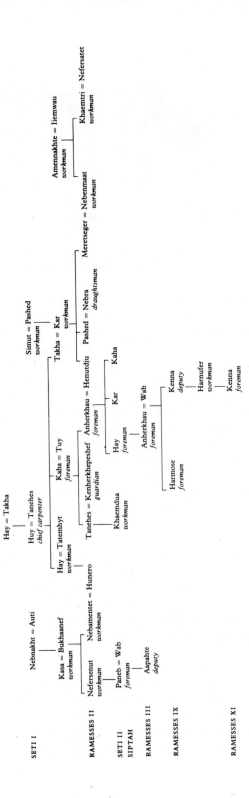

SETI I

RAMESSES II

SETI II
SIPTAH

RAMESSES III

RAMESSES IX

RAMESSES XI

INTERRELATIONSHIP PEDIGREE
This selection of individuals from the Deir el-Medina community shows the close connections which grew up between the various families in the village. The evidence is strongest in the reign of Ramesses II and is more patchy in the Twentieth Dynasty.

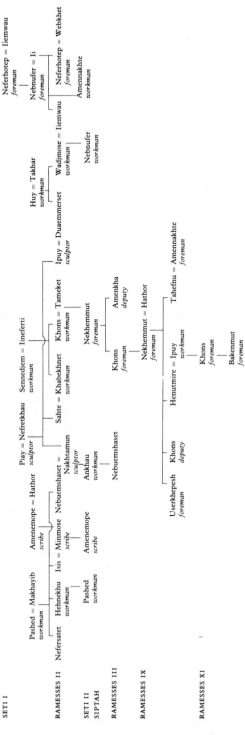

SETI I

RAMESSES II

SETI II
SIPTAH

RAMESSES III

RAMESSES IX

RAMESSES XI

50 (left) *Nursing scene. One of the chief occupations of the women of the village was, of course, the care of children. This ostracon depicts a women suckling a child, although she appears to be too elaborately dressed to have been an ordinary villager. Perhaps this illustrates a historical or mythological scene.*
51 (below) *Family group. This intimate scene from the tomb of the foreman Anherkhau shows a typical Deir el-Medina family.*

marriage from sharing the third of her matrimonial property. The disinherited children would still be eligible to share in the two-thirds of their father's matrimonial property:

She said: As for me, I am a free woman of the land of Pharaoh. I brought up these eight servants of yours and gave them a provision of everything as is usually made for those in their situation. But see I am grown old, and see, they are not looking after me in my turn. Whoever of them has aided me, to him I will give of my property but he who has not given to me, to him I will not give any of my property.

Later on in the document she became much more specific: 'List of her children of whom she said: They shall not participate in the division of my one-third, but in the two-thirds of their father they shall participate'. Four names of the disinherited children followed, but worse was to come:

As for these four children of mine, they shall not participate in the division of any of my property. And, as for the property of the scribe Kenherkhepeshef my first husband and also his landed property and this store-room of my father and also this measure of emmer which I collected in company with my husband, they shall not share them. As for these eight children of mine, they shall participate in the division of the property of their father in one single division.

Thus the ungrateful children were to be disinherited not only from their mother's third but also from her private property. All the children and her husband then swore to uphold the terms of Naunakhte's testament.

A marriage could, of course, be dissolved by divorce and not only by death. In ancient Egypt men and women were free to divorce their spouses if they so chose, but certain financial penalties were exacted. If a man repudiated his wife for any reason other than adultery, he was obliged to make a financial settlement on his ex-wife, rather like the modern concept of alimony except that in theory it would have been paid in one instalment, although in fact, it probably took the husband some time to raise the necessary capital. The amount was probably equivalent to the third of the marital property, plus a fine for repudiation except in cases where adultery was involved. In a dispute over the amount the local court would try to settle the matter. If a woman walked out on her husband, she too had to pay him compensation, but it was far less than he would be obliged to pay a repudiated wife. The woman's private property remained her own and she took it with her when she left the matrimonial home. If the house happened to belong to the wife by inheritance, then the husband had to leave, but otherwise the wife had no claim to remain in her ex-husband's home and presumably returned to her own family. The fate of the children of divorced couples is not clear. If they were adult, no problem arose. If minors, they may have gone with the wife, but this is not certain – they might conceivably have stayed with the father.

Family squabbles did not only involve husband and wife. The juvenile delinquent was not unknown to Deir el-Medina. The workman Menna had to put up with an extremely unsatisfactory son named Merysakhmet, alias Paroy. On one occasion, he quarrelled with the door-keeper Khaemwese when he took over his father's shift, and on another he was involved in a court case over some property which he lost. He was also accused of having an affair with a fellow workman's wife. At one stage he left the community and wandered about Egypt. Poor Menna wrote a long complaint about his son's behaviour, but it is uncertain what eventually became of him. High-spirited young men were doubtless a problem from time to time. One punishment for disobedience by workmen, young or old, was a sound thrashing. There is indeed a record of some workmen, who can be shown to be young men, receiving a beating for misdeeds.

Domestic discord would be all the more disturbing in the village of Deir el-Medina as, like most enclosed communities, everyone was related to everyone else. The illustrated pedigree shows an example of some of the close links which bound ordinary workmen, foremen and scribes together. Contrary to popular belief, the Egyptians did not marry their sisters except in the royal house. Wives were often termed sister as a title of respect but without any biological implications. Marriages of cousins were not unknown and there is a case of a marriage between an uncle and niece. There does not appear to be an obligatory pattern for naming children. In many cases, children were named for their grandparents or other close relations but rarely after their own parents. We know of numerous nicknames, such as 'The Wolf' or 'The Deputy'. In some cases there were standard diminutive forms for certain names, such as Hunero for Hathor or Ipuy for Amenemope. The ancestor cults practised at Deir el-Medina show that the members were keenly aware of the names of their forefathers. This knowledge is also reflected in the official records, as surviving fragments of a census of the village in the Twentieth Dynasty make clear. Each householder named not only his immediate family but also his parents:

House of Amennakhte son of Bukentef his mother being Tarekhanu
his wife Tentpaopet daughter of Khaemhedjet her mother being Tentkhenuemheb
his mother Tarekhanu daughter of Neferhotep her mother being Hatinufer

Another entry reads:

House of Ipuy son of Neferher his mother being Merutemmut
his wife Henutmire daughter of Nekhemmut her mother being Hathor
his daughter Henutnetjeru daughter of Ipuy her mother being Henutmire
his daughter Sebanufer daughter of Ipuy her mother being Henutmire
his daughter Hathor daughter of Ipuy her mother being Henutmire.

Life at Deir el-Medina was not all work; both men and women did find time to relax and enjoy themselves. The Egyptians were a fun-loving people who so much enjoyed the pleasures of life that they sought to continue these delights in the next life. Religious festivals were of course an

52 *The Turin Erotic Papyrus. While one section of this papyrus depicts erotic poses, another part contains satirical drawings of animals who are undertaking various mundane human activities.*

opportunity for the community to display emotion and celebration. There were more intimate occasions as well. Weddings, anniversaries and births could be celebrated with parties. Wine and beer would flow, while the guests were entertained by music and song. Presents were also exchanged, and it appears that careful lists were kept of who brought what so that the host and hostess could reciprocate with an equivalent gift at a future celebration. All parties were not necessarily innocent good fun. The Turin Erotic Papyrus, which undoubtedly comes from Deir el-Medina, depicts what might be called an orgy although it is not clear whether one couple is shown in several positions or several couples are taking part. If some of the accusations made in the community can be believed, adultery was a not uncommon form of recreation, but more innocent forms of amusement could be found in the home. The Egyptians possessed a number of games which could be played to pass the time, and pets might keep a worker amused, as well as performing vital functions in some cases: cats kept the rodent population at bay, although monkeys, baboons, and gazelles were purely decorative. A bored worker at home, or even on the job, could

53 *In this detail of a painting from the tomb of Nebenmaat, the deceased and his wife play a game of draughts.*

pass the time by sketching: large numbers of ostraca covered in designs have survived. Some of them were obviously trial pieces for larger works of art, but others are just plain doodles. They can depict gods, kings, men, women or animals, and ordinary activities of daily life are vividly represented. The Egyptians found it amusing to show animals performing human functions, often in reverse to their normal relationships, such as cats acting as servants to mice. One unique sketch can be recognized as a copy of an actual monument. This shows a fat lady who has plausibly been recognized as a version of the Queen of Punt depicted on the reliefs of the temple of Deir el-Bahri.

Literature, too, provided a distraction to members of the community. It was not only the scribes who were literate in Deir el-Medina. It is possible that a fairly substantial portion of the male inhabitants of the village was literate in hieratic if not hieroglyphic. The use of the hieroglyphic script at this time was restricted to monumental and decorative purposes on temples, tombs, stelae, coffins and votive objects, and was not for normal use. Everyday letters were written in hieratic, a shorthand version of hieroglyphic writing, so it was possible for an Egyptian to be literate in hieratic but not hieroglyphic. There is, indeed, some evidence from mistakes made in the writing of hieroglyphs that hieratic was the first basic script taught. Only the more advanced pupils went on to learn hieroglyphic. The draughtsmen and scribes at Deir el-Medina certainly knew both, but ordinary workmen are known to have written in hieratic without the aid of a scribe. The workman Amennakhte son of Khaemnun added a sentence in his own hand to a manuscript which he had ultimately inherited from his mother's first husband, the scribe Kenherkhepeshef. Numerous graffiti in hieratic and sometimes hieroglyphic show that the

54 (right) *Ostracon of a rooster, discovered in the Valley of the Kings. This may well have been the production of a bored workman.*

55 (below) *Ostracon with a sketch of a hefty woman who can probably be identified as the Queen of Punt from the reliefs of the temple of Queen Hatshepsut at Deir el-Bahri.*

56 (below right) *The Queen of Punt, a relief from the temple of Queen Hatshepsut.*

57 *The dream-book of Kenherkhepeshef. Amennakhte, son of Kenherkhepeshef's wife by her second marriage, eventually inherited the manuscript and his signature can be seen in the detail shown. Amennakhte calls himself a scribe, but it is known from other sources that he was an ordinary workman.*

ordinary workmen could certainly write their own names. If they could write, then they no doubt could read.

It is not clear where such knowledge was acquired. The sons of scribes and draughtsmen would have been taught by their fathers, but it is probable that there may have been larger classes involving the sons of ordinary workmen. The workmen's children may have attended only sporadically or been forced to drop out eventually due to economic pressures, but it is likely that their fathers would have tried to ensure that their sons acquired as much learning as possible to enable them perhaps to rise in the world if the opportunity occurred. The posts of scribes and draughtsmen would normally have been filled from the same families, so a talented member of another family might have had to leave the community if he wished to get on. Indeed, the son of the chief workman Neferhotep the elder became an army scribe.

The reading tastes of the average literate Egyptian of the time are revealed by the literary legacy of Deir el-Medina. The compositions were written on papyri or ostraca. It used to be thought that papyrus was expensive, but a recent study has shown that it was relatively cheap and well within a workman's budget. In a number of cases, the remains from Deir el-Medina constitute the sole evidence for the existence of certain literary pieces. Many literary ostraca remain unpublished, but the broad outlines of the literary history of the community can be drawn from over 1500 published examples. These often comprise only a few lines of a text, and several different ostraca might originally have been part of the same copy. A few might have been school texts, but the majority seem to have been produced for private use. Sometimes complete copies of a work are available elsewhere on papyrus, but gaps and problems of interpretation still remain which can sometimes be solved by the Deir el-Medina texts.

The most numerous group of texts is that now called wisdom literature.

This genre of literature consisted of moral precepts and advice on behaviour offered by learned scribes, officials and even kings. The writers
of the wisdom texts were admired and remembered through the ages:

Is there one here like Hordjedef? Is there another like Imhotep? There have been
none among our kindred like Neferti and Khety, that chief among them. I recall to
you the names of Ptahemdjedhuty and Khakheperreseneb. Is there another like
Ptahhotpe or like Kaires?

The earliest text of this nature was supposed to have been written by the
celebrated vizier Imhotep (*c.* 2650 BC), but not a sentence of this has
survived. Fragments of the text of Hordjedef son of Khufu (*c.* 2550 BC)
are known solely from Deir el-Medina. Several of the other authors are
known from examples at Deir el-Medina and elsewhere, while others may
be represented in several of the anonymous wisdom texts which have come
down to us without their opening lines. The most frequent work on
ostraca from the site is the famous *Satire on Trades* by the author Khety.
This text ridicules all professions except that of scribe, to which all are
encouraged to aspire. Khety also was the ghost-writer of the *Instructions
of King Amenemhat I*, supposedly a didactic work by the king but actually
composed after his assassination in 1962 BC. As this piece is the second
most popular found at Deir el-Medina, Khety must be considered the
best-selling author of the second millenium BC. Papyri and ostraca from
Deir el-Medina were until recently practically the sole evidence for the
Maxims of Any, a work of the Eighteenth Dynasty, but a copy has now
turned up at Saqqara.

Apart from wisdom literature, the average Egyptian might be entertained by popular stories, and several examples have been found at Deir
el-Medina. One of the best known is the tale of the adventures of Sinuhe,
an Egyptian political refugee in Palestine during the reign of Senwosret I
(*c.* 1960 BC). This text has survived in full from other sites, but Deir el-
Medina has yielded both fragments and a complete version of the story
which is written on the largest ostracon yet known, measuring 88.5 cm
high and 31.5 cm wide. It is now in the Ashmolean Museum, Oxford.
Other tales which are found at Deir el-Medina concern the activities of the
gods, such as the adventures of Seth and Anat and a complete papyrus of
the *Contendings of Horus and Seth*. There is also the allegorical tale of the
Blinding of Truth by Falsehood, of which only one incomplete copy from
Deir el-Medina survives. The hero Truth is wrongly accused of theft by
his wicked brother Falsehood and blinded by order of the gods. Falsehood orders his servants to throw his brother to the lions, but they take
pity on the blind Truth and do not carry out the command. They inform
Falsehood that the order has been carried out. Truth is discovered lying
in a ditch by the servants of a lady who gives him the post of door-keeper
in her household. Because Truth is so handsome, she sleeps with him and

58 *The Ashmolean ostracon of Sinuhe. The largest ostracon known, it contains on both sides the text of the adventures of Sinuhe, a courtier of Senwosret I. Although written in the Middle Kingdom, the story remained popular in Ramesside times, and numerous late copies have survived.*

bears him a son. The boy is not told who his father is. He grows up and excels in school so his jealous schoolmates taunt him about his lack of a father. He demands to know who his father is, and his mother admits that he is the door-keeper of her household. The boy is furious at the treatment accorded to his father, whom he immediately places at the seat of honour at the table. He also determines to avenge the sufferings of his father. He tricks his wicked uncle into a virtual admission that his original story of the theft was false. Falsehood is then sentenced to be beaten and blinded and placed as door-keeper at the house of Truth.

The literary legacy of Deir el-Medina also includes a number of examples of hymns to various deities, poems in honour of certain kings, and magical texts which are largely unique. The celebrated dream-book of Kenherkhepeshef is one important such text. Another useful compilation was a papyrus of spells against scorpions: the danger of scorpions was ever present at Deir el-Medina as the attendance register makes clear. Another collection of spells was meant to offer protection for people on the river, and yet another lists spells intended to increase sexual potency. The Turin Papyrus is not the sole remains of eroticism at Deir el-Medina; apart from a number of illustrated ostraca, there are also love-poems on papyrus and ostraca. Several of these had been inscribed on a pot, but that was eventually broken. However, some fragments were found at the end of the last century and more during the French excavations of this century, and although the text is by no means complete, some of it can now be reconstructed. The beloved is addressed by the term of sister, a token of respect and honour:

My sister has come, my heart is exultant
My arms spread out to embrace her
As for my heart, it is overjoyed in its place like a fish in its pond
O night may you last an eternity for me
Now that my lady has come.

Thus the members of the community led full and varied lives. Hard work was compensated by pleasures of the spirit and the body. It was fashionable in the early part of this century to consider the workmen and their families as poor or proletarian. It is obvious from a description of their lifestyle that their lot was far above that of the average peasant, although it might not aspire to the level of the aristocracy. The workmen were, in good times, amply paid in goods and services for their labour. Naturally there were social variations in the village, but even the ordinary workman had the opportunity and means to live well.

59 *Ramesside chapels at Deir el-Medina. These chapels are now situated within the enclosure wall of the later Ptolemaic temple.*

5 Religion

RELIGION PLAYED an important and intimate role in the daily life of the worker's community. Several large temples stood to the north and northeast of the village proper, and the cliff face near the village was dotted with chapels to the various gods. More chapels still were situated in the cliffs between the village and the Valley of the Kings, and in the Valley of the Queens. The temples and chapels would have been filled with stelae, statues and offering-tables dedicated to the resident deity, although some objects were not just dedicated to the gods in whose chapels they were placed. Many of the chapels cannot be assigned to a known god at present, while some deities seem to have a number of chapels dedicated to them. The Egyptians were a practical people and not much inclined to philosophical theology, and they never tried to work out a systematic relationship for their many gods to be applied over the whole country. In prehistoric times each village would appear to have had its local deity. With the union of the country some minor gods were absorbed by their more powerful neighbours, while others continued to live peacefully beside imported new ones. Some divinities became recognized throughout the country because of the patronage of the court and the influence of their priesthood. There were local attempts to organize divinities in triads, consisting of a divine couple with child, but all these local triads were never brought together into a grand framework. Only the most powerful priesthoods, such as that of Ptah of Memphis or Re of Heliopolis, tried to formulate a standard theology, but its use was restricted to the clergy of those temples and had little impact on the ordinary individual.

Re, the sun-god, had been elevated to the position of chief deity through the patronage of the rulers of the Fifth Dynasty, but the kings of the Eighteenth Dynasty who founded Deir el-Medina followed a different god, Amun of Thebes. The triumphs of these rulers in war, and the riches that they bestowed on Amun's temples and clergy, assured his elevation to national supremacy. He absorbed the old national god Re and was thus transformed into Amen-Re, king of the gods. His main temple was at Karnak on the east bank of the Nile near Thebes under the charge of the high priest and a numerous clergy. He, his wife Mut, and his son

60 *Stela of the workman Nefersenut. The workman kneels with a brazier containing an offering before the goddess Hathor. Below, his sons kneel in adoration. His eldest son Paneb was to rise to the post of foreman of the workmen.*

Khons formed the Theban triad of divinities, worshipped in the Theban area and beyond. There was needless to say a temple dedicated to Amun at Deir el-Medina. It seems to have originally been erected in the Eighteenth Dynasty but was considerably rebuilt and enlarged in the reign of Ramesses II. The majority of the stelae, which can be identified as coming from Deir el-Medina, are dedicated to him as Amun or Amen-Re.

Seti I erected a large chapel to the cow-goddess Hathor north of the village. This goddess was especially popular on the west bank of the Nile, where the Deir el-Bahri temples were devoted to her cult. The workmen would have been familiar with her shrine at Deir el-Bahri, as it was located just on the other side of the cliff from the Valley of the Kings. Hathor was regarded as a goddess of love and fertility but also as a sky-goddess and a divine nurse to kings. She was sometimes considered a daughter of Amen-

61 *Statue of the workman Penmerneb. The workman carries an image of the god Amen-Re, who is often portrayed in the form of a ram.*

62 *Worship of the goddess Meretseger. This finely painted
ostracon unfortunately lacks the name of the devotee,
as the stone is broken away in the crucial area.*

Re, but at other times she was thought of as his mother. Many of the
stelae set up in her name must have come from her temple. In the Ptolemaic
period her association with Deir el-Medina led to the construction of the
great temple to Hathor which has endured to this day. Travellers in the
eighteenth and early nineteenth centuries mistakenly identified it as a
temple to Isis, another female divinity.

In the temple of Hathor excavation has uncovered the statue of another
female divinity who was sometimes identified as a form of Hathor – the
snake-goddess Meretseger. Her cult was a particularly local worship and
was especially strong at Deir el-Medina. She was associated with the great
peak, now known as El-Qurn, which dominated the west bank area and
whose slope was covered in shrines. She was often depicted in the guise of
a cobra, of which there must have been numerous living examples on the
west bank. Meretseger was also commemorated in a sanctuary built for the
god Ptah on the road to the Valley of the Queens. This appears to have
been founded at the beginning of the Twentieth Dynasty, but fragments
of stelae from the Nineteenth Dynasty may indicate that it was even
earlier. The sanctuary consists of a series of rock-cut chapels in the face
of the cliff. The god Ptah, who originally came from Memphis, was
regarded as the patron of craftsmen and the lord of righteousness and
many of the stelae erected in his name probably were set up in one of these
chapels.

The cult of Osiris and Isis is better represented in the tombs than on
the stelae. As lord of the underworld and protector of the dead, Osiris

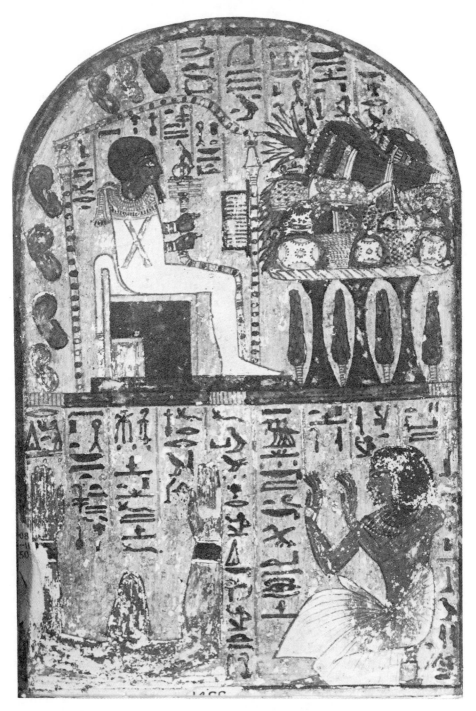

63 *Stela of the guardian Penbuy. The god Ptah is seated in his kiosk before a large heap of offerings. Behind are many ears so that he could hear better the prayer of the dedicatee. Below, Penbuy worships the spirit of Ptah.*

was more naturally invoked in a funerary context. Worship of his wife Isis seems to have been eclipsed by the other powerful female cults at Deir el-Medina. Among the other deities which appear on monuments and stelae and in tombs are the ram-headed god Khnum, a creator god from Elephantine, and his female associates Anuket and Satet; Anubis, the jackal-headed god of embalming; Taweret, the hippopotamus-goddess of child-birth; Re-Harakhty, a hawk-headed solar deity; and the ibis-headed Thoth, patron of the scribal arts. Foreign Asiatic divinities, which were popular in Egypt in the New Kingdom, also make their appearance at Deir el-Medina. These include Reshep, a war god, and the

64 (left) *The god Osiris from the tomb of Sennedjem.*

65 (right) *Stela of the foreman Kaha. The Asiatic goddess Qudshu is depicted in the upper register on top of a lion. On the right is the Asiatic god Reshep and on the left the Egyptian fertility god Min. Below, Kaha and his family worship another Asiatic goddess, Anat.*

fertility goddesses Qudshu, Anat, and Astarte. A popular Egyptian god, Bes, depicted as a bearded dwarf, is associated with amulets and frescoes found in the village. His principal function was as a god of fertility, but he was also concerned with dance and music.

The Egyptians not only worshipped gods but also deified kings and other mortals. One of the most important religious centres in the community was the temple dedicated to the deified king Amenhotpe I and his mother Ahmes-Nefertari. He was regarded as the patron of the village, possibly because he had founded the corps of workmen. He appears on many stelae and in tombs, where he is sometimes shown with other

66 (left) *Wooden statue of Queen Ahmes-Nefertari. Worship of this queen was coupled with that of her son Amenhotpe I. This statue was dedicated by the workman Wadjmose in the reign of Ramessess II (c. 1279–1212 BC).*

67 (right) *The cult of Amenhotpe I. This painted statue probably came from his temple at Deir el-Medina. Early Egyptologists were misled into dating many of the Deir el-Medina monuments to his reign until it was realized that he was worshipped as a god many generations after his death.*

members of his large family of brothers and sisters, such as the young
Prince Sipair, who appears to have died in his youth. It is not always clear
that the Ramesside workers understood the genealogical ramifications of
the royal family which flourished about three hundred years before. Some
of the royal names and relationships are definitely garbled. The popularity
of Amenhotpe I is even more unusual as it appears that it was his successor
Thutmose I who actually founded the village. Thutmose I was not a son of
his predecessor and it is probable that Amenhotpe I left no descendants.
Other rulers of the Eighteenth, Nineteenth and Twentieth Dynasties are
depicted on stelae and reliefs either as objects of a cult in their own right
or as intercessors between the workmen and the gods. There definitely
was a chapel dedicated to Ramesses II, and there may have been other
chapels to other kings.

68 (left) *Stela of Any. The deceased workman is portrayed as an excellent spirit of Re. Stelae of this kind were probably set up in houses as part of the ancestor cult.*
69 (right) *Stela with ancestral busts. Two small busts are attached to the top while below the dedicatee, whose name is lost, worships another bust. This stela undoubtedly comes from Deir el-Medina.*

Much more interesting are the stelae which were dedicated to the memory of deceased members of the community. Some of these were erected in the houses from which they have been recovered in the course of excavation, while others may have been placed in chapels. The departed were styled as 'excellent spirits of Re'. The stelae on which they appear are rounded or pointed at the top and appear to have been designed to fit into special niches. The deceased is named quite simply without any indication of position or family. He is most often shown seated and holding a lotus blossom. Sometimes more than one departed spirit is depicted, but the relationship between them is not specified. In one tomb a foreman Neferhotep is depicted with the title of 'excellent spirit of Re' and is being honoured, if not worshipped, by the tomb-owner and his family. It is

95

Religion

70 *Relief of the workman Meriwese. This relief depicts a religious occasion in the village when the image of a deity, in this case Amun, was carried in procession. Several workmen act the part of priests holding the divine bark.*

interesting that no relationship is known between Neferhotep and the tomb-owner. Dedications to deceased relations also appear on offering-tables. It seems that this cult of the 'excellent spirits of Re' was connected with that of the solar god Harmakhis. Apart from this particular form of ancestor worship, the members of the community also had ancestral busts of their relations in their houses. This veneration of the departed generations within the home may not have been unique to Deir el-Medina, and probably was common to all Egyptian homes, but from nowhere else is the evidence clearer to interpret than at Deir el-Medina.

With such a multiplicity of divinities and temples, the community might be thought to have required a large number of priests to serve its needs. This was not, however, the case. The workmen themselves acted as their own priests and performed all the sacred rituals for their gods. Possibly the same daily religious ceremonies which were enacted in the main temples would be carried out there. The image of the god would be clothed and offered food, although the richness of the clothes and food would naturally be somewhat less in Deir el-Medina than in the main temple at Karnak. On festival days the workers would be transformed into *wab*-priests, 'pure of hands', and carry the image of the god in procession through the village and probably beyond. The important gods did not just have one feast day but many. Amenhotpe I had at least seven, one of which entailed several days' drinking and rejoicing. Not all such occasions, however, were festive, as the religious calendar also included days of mourning and meditation. The community would presumably also take part in the great religious festivals in which the whole of the west bank participated, such as the Feast of the Valley, when the sacred image of the god Amun of Karnak was brought across the river to visit the mortuary temples of the deceased rulers.

The temples and chapels at Deir el-Medina would have been filled with stelae and offering-tables with prayers on behalf of the donors. In many cases these were the simple standard formulae found on similar monuments from other parts of Egypt:

A boon which the king gives to Amen-Re, lord of the thrones of the two lands, and Mut, the great, lady of the two lands and mistress of all the gods that they cause my name to be firm in the place of Truth like Truth itself for the spirit of the servant in the place of Truth Parennufer justified beautiful in rest.

Or:

Giving praise to the good god lord of the two lands Djeserkare son of Re, lord of diadems, Amenhotpe, given life, who kisses the ground, and to the King's Mother and King's Great Wife Ahmes-Nefertari, may she live, that they give life, prosperity, and health to the spirit of the chief workman in the Place of Truth Neferhotep justified son of the chief workman Nebnufer justified beautiful in rest.

However, not all the prayers are the stereotyped expressions that are normally associated with Egyptian funerary monuments. Several stelae appear to have been carved and erected in response to specific situations for which the donor wishes to thank the god or goddess concerned. The draughtsman Nebre set up a stela to honour Amen-Re for curing his son Nakhtamun:

I made praises to his name
Because of the greatness of his power.
I made prayers before him
In the presence of the whole land,
For the draughtsman Nakhtamun, justified,
Who lay sick unto death
Under the might of Amun on account of his sin . . .

I will make this stela in your name,
And record this prayer in writing on it,
For you saved for me the draughtsman Nakhtamun.
So I said to you and you heard me . . .

The workman Neferabu set up two stelae, one to Meretseger and the second to Ptah, both of which probably came from the sanctuary to Ptah on the road to the Valley of the Queens. The prayers on both are surprisingly similar although they appear to refer to different incidents:

97

I was an ignorant and foolish man
Who did not know good from evil.
I sinned against the Peak
And she taught me a lesson.
I was in her power night and day . . .
I called to my Lady.
She came to me as a sweet breeze.
She was merciful to me
After she had caused me to see her power.
She turned to me again in peace;
She made me forget the illness which I had suffered.
Lo, the Peak of the West is appeased
If one calls upon her.
Spoken by Neferabu justified.
He says: Behold, let every ear hear
That lives upon earth:
Beware of the Peak of the West.

I was a man who swore falsely by Ptah, Lord of Truth,
And he caused me to see darkness by day.
I will declare his might to the ignorant and the knowing,
To the little and the great.
Beware of Ptah, Lord of Truth.
Lo, he will not overlook anyone's deed.
Refrain from uttering the name of Ptah falsely.
He who utters it falsely will fall . . .

It would seem that on the onset of illness, Neferabu would remember his faults and, on his recovery, set up a memorial to the divinity whom he believed that he had offended and who had forgiven his offence and helped to cure him. It may not be amiss to point out that Neferabu's father-in-law was in fact the village doctor, who may have played some part in Neferabu's miracle cures.

The Egyptian gods were not aloof and distant but played a direct part in the life of the community. On important matters a god could be consulted by oracle. The use of oracles is well attested at the great temples such as Karnak, where the god decided such questions as the appointment of his priests. At Deir el-Medina the deified Amenhotpe I is known to have been consulted by oracle. These consultations were concerned with claims to property and not offices. When the ruling of the civil court was disputed, or, if it was not involved, the god could be called upon to render a decision. During the oracular consultation, the image of the god was borne by the workman-priests before the petitioner. He would state his case and possibly this would be repeated by the scribe of the Tomb. The god would then indicate his decision. The surviving records imply that the god delivered a lengthy address on the question, but this is probably due to the official method of recording the verdict of the oracle. It is more

71 *The prayer of Neferabu. This prayer of repentence is inscribed on the back of a stela dedicated to the god Ptah, lord of righteousness, whom Neferabu had offended.*

likely that the god answered specific questions in the positive or negative or indicated which of two written petitions he favoured. The bearers, and hence the divine image, would no doubt move to one side or another, or possibly up or down, to signify approval or disapproval. The bearers would of course be moved by divine intervention, although they probably had an opinion as to the justice of the claims of the petitioner. The workman Amenemope made a claim to own a certain tomb and was confirmed in his ownership by the god: 'Year 21 [of Ramesses III, *c.* 1166 BC], second month of Shomu, day 1, I stood before Amenhotpe saying to him: "Give me a tomb among the ancestors." He gave me the tomb of Hay in writing.' For unknown reasons the judgement of the god was not necessarily considered final in some instances, as there is evidence that court proceedings followed one oracular decision.

The Egyptians did not regard their gods as always awe-inspiring, remote deities. Like the Greeks, they conceived of the gods as having human desires and foibles. This facet of Egyptian religion is reflected in popular folk tales about the gods and their activities. The longest and

99

most interesting of the surviving tales is *The Contendings of Horus and Seth*, which is preserved, along with other texts, on a magnificent papyrus roll undoubtedly from Deir el-Medina, now in the Chester Beatty Library in Dublin. The story deals with the claim of the god Horus, son of Osiris and Isis, to succeed to his father's throne. Osiris had previously been King of Egypt, but had been murdered by his brother Seth and then transformed into the King of the Underworld. Horus's right to succeed his father was opposed by his uncle Seth, who desired the throne for himself. When the tale commences, the divine council, or Ennead, under the presidency of the supreme god Re or Re-Harakhty had been debating the issue for eighty years but had reached no decision. The majority on the council favoured Horus, but Re wished to give the office to his favourite son Seth. After an acrimonious opening debate, the council decided to seek the advice of the mother-goddess Neith. She replied by letter that the office should be given to Horus, but Seth should be compensated with a doubling of his possessions and the hands of the goddesses Anat and Astarte, daughters of Re:

Then Thoth read it out before the Lord of All and the entire Ennead. They declared in unison: 'This goddess is right.' Then the Lord of All became angry at Horus and said to him: 'You are weak in your limbs. This office is too great for you, youngster whose breath is foul.' Then Onuris became exceedingly angry and so was the entire Ennead consisting of the Council of Thirty. Then the god Baba arose and said to Re-Harakhty: 'Your shrine is empty'. Re-Harakhty was offended by the answer which was spoken to him. He lay down on his back with a very sore heart.

The council broke up, while its leader sulked. Fortunately the gods soon thought of a way to cheer Re up:

The great god spent a day lying on his back in his pavilion. After a long while, Hathor, Lady of the Southern Sycamore, came and stood in front of her father, the Lord of All. She uncovered her private parts before him. Then the great god laughed at her. He arose and sat with the great Ennead.

The divine bickering continued. Isis threatened to appeal to yet higher gods and was assured that justice would be done, whereupon Seth lost his temper. He threatened to kill the members of the court and refused to take part in any further proceedings until Isis was excluded. Re then moved the proceedings to an island and ordered Nemty the ferryman not to convey Isis across to it. The determined goddess simply disguised herself as an old crone sporting a gold signet ring. She asked Nemty to ferry her across in order to bring food to a youth who was looking after cattle on the island. The ferryman agreed to do so in return for her gold ring. Once over, Isis prepared a trap for the unsuspecting Seth by transforming herself yet again, this time into a beautiful maiden. The beauty immediately attracted the attention of the lusty Seth. In reply to his eager salutation, she declared:

As for me, I was the wife of a herdsman. I bore him a son. Then my husband died. The youngster began to look after the cattle of his father. Then a stranger came and sat down in my stable. He said thus to my son: 'I shall beat you, I shall seize the cattle of your father, and I shall throw you out.' Thus he spoke to him. It is my wish that you act as a champion for him. Then Seth said to her: 'Shall the cattle be given to a stranger while a son of the owner exists?' Then Isis changed herself into a kite and flew up and sat on the top of an acacia tree. She called out to Seth and said to him: 'Weep for yourself. It is your own mouth which has said it. It is your own cleverness which has judged you.'

This exchange had much more meaning for an Egyptian reader, as the words for cattle and office are synonyms in ancient Egyptian. The reader would have appreciated the pun. Seth, of course, had now condemned his actions out of his own mouth. He complained bitterly to Re about Isis's presence. Nemty the ferryman was punished for his greed. Seth then challenged Horus to a duel for the office of king. Both gods turned into hippopotami and began to fight in the water. Isis, never willing to leave matters to chance, immediately seized a harpoon and flung it into the water. Unfortunately, she hit Horus who cried out in pain. The weapon was withdrawn. At her second attempt she harpooned Seth, but she was moved by her brother's plea and let go of him. Horus was furious. He

72 The Contendings of Horus and Seth. *The story is written in hieratic, a short-hand version of hieroglyphic used for writing on payri and ostraca. The text is in black ink except at the beginning of paragraphs where the first few letters are in red.*

jumped out of the water, decapitated his mother, and fled into the mountains. The Ennead pursued. Seth found him and blinded him, but he was rescued by Hathor who restored his eyesight.

The Ennead then ordered the two gods to stop quarrelling. In a spirit of reconciliation Seth invited Horus to his house for the evening. During the night the wicked Seth raped his nephew. Horus then complained to his mother, now apparently restored to health and back in the fight. Isis first disposed of Seth's sperm. She then took some of Horus's and smeared it on a lettuce, one of Seth's favourite foods. He ate it without suspecting that anything was amiss. At the next court appearance, Seth denounced Horus:

Then Seth said: 'Let the office of ruler be given to me, for as regards Horus who is standing here, I have acted the part of a man against him.' Then the Ennead let out a great cry. They belched and spat before Horus. Then Horus laughed at them. Then Horus swore an oath by the god, saying: 'All that Seth has spoken is false. Let the sperm of Seth be summoned and we shall see from where it shall answer. Let my own be summoned and we shall see from where it shall answer.'

The Egyptians apparently viewed the passive partner in a homosexual relationship with distaste and Horus would have been disgraced if Seth's charge could have been proved. However, when summoned Seth's sperm was found to be in a marsh, while that of Horus emerged from Seth's forehead in the form of a golden disk.

Seth still refused to give way to Horus. He challenged his nephew to a naval combat. Seth stupidly built a boat of stone which immediately sank. Horus now lost patience and journeyed to the goddess Neith to demand justice. An acrimonious correspondence then ensued between the Ennead and Horus's father Osiris, ruler of the underworld. Osiris threatened to have the gods dragged into the underworld unless justice was done. Then the Ennead proclaimed Horus ruler of earth, while Seth was compensated by being made lord of thunder in the sky.

The above tale does not depict the gods in a particularly flattering light. They are shown as liars, cheats, bickering among themselves, and subject to the human faults of greed and lust. There were no doubt equally ribald stories of the gods and even of the kings which have not survived in detail. However, the gods may have appealed to the workmen for these very informal qualities. The grand temples and the austere priesthood are but one aspect of the ancient Egyptian religion, and the lively personal interaction between the gods and man can be seen to better advantage at Deir el-Medina than at the temples of Karnak and Luxor.

6 Justice

THE LIFE OF any small community does not always run smoothly. Disputes or even violence may break out among its members, and the village of Deir el-Medina was no exception. In order to settle any disagreements the community possessed its own court, known as the *kenbet*, composed of the officers of the village – the foremen, deputies and scribes – plus certain ordinary village members who may have been co-opted to serve on the court due to their seniority or esteem in the village. Its sessions may have taken place on rest days when the men were not at work in the royal tomb, or possibly sometimes in the evenings, when the men were at ease in the Valley of the Kings. The court had the power to settle all civil action and even to decide minor criminal matters, but major cases involving capital offences were referred to the vizier's court at Thebes.

The bulk of the cases tried by the court seem to have consisted of disputes over non-payment for goods and services. The members of the community appeared to have enjoyed a good court case, which was no doubt a diversion from the general routine, and were quite prepared to go to law for what may seem trifling matters. The expense was not very great, for it appears that each man or woman conducted their own case and so lawyers' fees were not required. One action, although this may not be typical, was the attempt by the workman Menna to recover payment owed to him for a pot of fat which he had sold on credit. He was not at all deterred by the fact that the defaulter was the chief of police Mentmose:

Year 17 . . . under the Majesty of the King of Upper and Lower Egypt . . . Ramesses [III, *c.* 1170 BC]. On that day the workman Menna gave the pot of fresh fat to the chief of police Mentmose who said: I will pay for it in barley . . . May Re keep you in health. So he said to me. I have reported him three times in the court before the scribe of the Tomb Amennakhte, but he has not given me anything to this day. Behold, I have reported him to him in year 3, second month of the summer season day 5 of the Majesty of the King of Upper and Lower Egypt . . . Ramesses [IV], that is eighteen years later. He took an oath by the Lord, saying: If I do not pay him for his pot before year 3, third month of the summer season, last day, I shall receive a hundred blows of the stick and shall be liable to pay double . . .

There is additional evidence that Menna and Mentmose were involved in

Justice

yet another court battle over non-payment for some articles of clothing, an action which seems to have gone on for about eleven years. Moreover, Menna is also on record in year 28 of Ramesses III suing the water-carrier Tcha for selling him a defective donkey. Menna won his case and Tcha was ordered by the court to either return the payment or supply a better donkey. Clearly Menna was a dangerous man to cross.

However, the decision of the court in such matters was not always final. There was always the difficulty of forcing the debtor to pay. The door-keepers of the Tomb were employed by the court to exact payments due, but there is one recorded case when the enraged debtor turned on the bailiff and gave him a thrashing without paying up. The example of Mentmose shows that payments could be avoided for long periods of time despite legal sentence. If a loser disagreed with the court's decision or a claimant preferred not to trust human judges, it was also possible to appeal to the gods. The deified king Amenhotpe I could be asked to render an oracular verdict on any claims submitted to him, and any decision would be backed by religious as well as legal force.

The court also possessed a notarial function, as deeds of gift or divisions of property were registered with the court, presumably to prevent any future disputes. In year 3 of Ramesses V (*c.* 1146 BC) the lady Naunakhte made a declaration concerning the future disposal of her property before a court which consisted of the foreman Nekhemmut, the foreman An-herkhau, the scribe of the Tomb Amennakhte, the scribe Harshire, the draughtsman Amenhotpe, the workman Telmont, the workman To, the draughtsman Pentaweret, the workman Userhat, the workman Nebnufer, the workman Amenpahapi, the district officer Amennakhte, the district officer Ramose, and the workman Nebnufer son of Khons. It appears to have been a packed session. The lady lay down the division of her property as she saw fit, and her husband and children swore to abide by her wishes. The proceedings were carefully recorded on papyrus so there could be no future dispute. It does not appear that the court itself kept any archives which recorded its decisions. These would have been kept by the interested parties to be produced in the event of future proceedings. However, some previous decisions were remembered, no doubt because they concerned certain *causes célèbres*. These might be invoked as precedents when required. Not all property was divided as clearly as that of the lady Naunakhte, so that family squabbles over property were not unknown to the judges of the community.

Apart from lawsuits over debt and property, the court also dealt with more serious offences such as theft. A notable trial took place in year 6 of Seti II (*c.* 1197 BC) when the workman Nebnufer son of Nakhy appeared before the court and accused the lady Heria of stealing a valuable tool which he had buried in his house. He does not explain why he buried it, but, as it is probable that a few years before Thebes may have been

73 (right) *Stela of Kenherkhepeshef, son of Naunakhte. The workman kneels in prayer to the goddess Mut, wife of Amun. The text is very crudely incised. It names his family, including a daughter Naunakhte, no doubt called after her grandmother.*

74 (below) *The will of Naunakhte. This papyrus formed part of the documentation drawn up on behalf of the lady Naunakhte in order to set down the division of her property which she wished to take place on her death. The two columns on the right contain the names of the presiding workmen.*

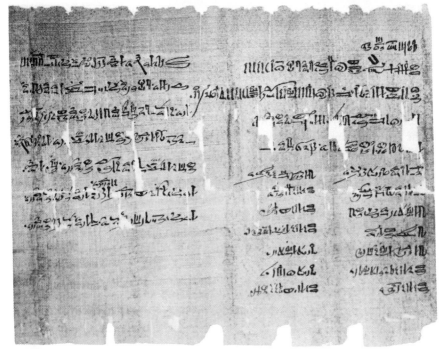

75 *The trial of Heria. This ostracon, which is inscribed on both sides, records the trial and eventual conviction of the lady Heria for theft and perjury.*

engulfed in a civil war between rival pharaohs, such a precaution may have been necessary. The owner appears to have left the village temporarily, no doubt due to the disturbances, and on his return the tool was gone. He questioned various members of the community and eventually accused Heria of this crime:

The court then examined Heria. Did you steal the tool of Nebnufer? True or false. What Heria said: No, I did not steal it. The tribunal then asked her: Can you swear a solemn oath by the Lord about the tool, saying I did not steal it.

Heria immediately took the required oath in the name of the god Amun.

However, in this case, the court did not rely simply on the word of the accused. A workman was sent to search her house. He discovered not only the missing tool but also ritual equipment stolen from the local temple. The lady was not only guilty of theft, but also of perjury and blasphemy. The court immediately declared Heria 'worthy of death'. However, in such criminal cases, the court could only decide guilt or innocence but could not enforce capital punishment. The whole matter was remitted to the vizier for his final judgement. Needless to say, we do not know the final verdict on the lady Heria. The same ostracon which records her case mentions as a precedent the fate of another lady thief in the reign of Ramesses II. The lady Tanedjemhemes, wife of the workman Pashed son of Heh, was found guilty of stealing a vase: 'The vizier had the scribe Hatiay come. He had her taken to the river bank'. It is not at all clear what the last phrase means. It has been interpreted either as a reference to a place of imprisonment or, more likely, to the transport of the guilty party across the Nile to the vizier's court at Thebes, from which she never returned to the village.

A case of blasphemy with potentially far more dangerous consequences had been tried only a year before in the community. In year 5 of Seti II the foreman Hay was brought before the tribunal which was presided over by his fellow foreman Paneb. Relations between the two were not the best, as Paneb was reported to have threatened to kill Hay. Four villagers declared that Hay 'had pronounced insults against Seti'. Seti was, of course, the Pharaoh, and an attack on his person was equivalent to sacrilege. Hay declared in his defence that at the time of the alleged crime he was fast asleep. The court then inquired into the nature of the alleged insults, but at this point the accusers became mysteriously silent and declared that they had heard nothing at all. They were then required to swear that they were not hiding anything, and nothing had been said against Pharaoh. They were further sentenced to receive a hundred blows each for bearing false witness. This case is distinctly odd. Was it merely the action of a few disgruntled villagers who were trying to get even with the boss, but then lost their nerve at the last moment? It must be remembered that Seti II may have recently regained power in Thebes after a civil disturbance. The accusation of blasphemy against his name might have implied that Hay was a supporter of the recently defeated rival. If so, he would have been in obvious danger of dismissal, or even harsher punishment, when his partiality was proved. Could perhaps the accusers been put up to their charge by Hay's enemies, such as his fellow foreman Paneb? That is probably a far-fetched speculation. It is even possible that Hay was guilty, but the witnesses against him were too frightened to proceed with their accusations. At any rate, Hay continued as chief workman for another thirty years, presumably died in his bed, and passed his office on to his son.

Paneb's career, however, appears to have ended more dramatically. Our knowledge of Paneb's crimes stems almost entirely from a petition drawn up towards the end of the Nineteenth Dynasty – the famous Salt papyrus, named after its first owner in modern times, Henry Salt. The petition which we now possess is either a copy of the original which was sent to the higher authorities, or it is the original which was never sent off. In view of the later action taken against Paneb, it may be presumed that some sort of complaint did eventually reach the vizier's office. It was, of course, open to all members of the community, or indeed any Egyptian, to petition directly to the vizier, but considering his close links with the workmen's community, complaints from the workmen themselves would more likely receive more immediate attention. The petition was drawn up by the workman Amennakhte, son of the chief workman Nebnufer and brother of the foreman Neferhotep; he was an embittered man, so his accusations against Paneb must be seen in this light. Amennakhte felt

76 *The Salt Papyrus, which contains the petition of the workman Amennakhte denouncing the crimes of the foreman Paneb. He demands that Paneb be removed from office and he be replaced by the rightful foreman, namely himself.*

aggrieved that he had not been made foreman and demanded that justice be done and his brother's position be given to him as heir of the family:

I am the son of the chief workman Nebnufer. My father died and the chief workman Neferhotep my brother was put in his place. The enemy killed Neferhotep, and, although I was his brother, Paneb gave five servants of my father to Preemheb who was then vizier . . . and he put him in the place of my father although indeed it was not his place.

However, Amennakhte is later forced to admit that Paneb did have a tenuous right to the job. Although only the son of the workman Nefersenut, Paneb was brought up by the childless Neferhotep as his foster-son, although according to Amennakhte they soon became estranged. Indeed, in a graffito found in the Theban hills, Paneb names Neferhotep as his father. If he had at some point been legally adopted by Neferhotep, then he certainly had a strong claim to the position of chief workman. It is curious, that, while denouncing him for handing over several household slaves, which Neferhotep presumably had inherited from his father, Amennakhte does not deny that Paneb had some legal right of ownership over them. As the adopted son of Neferhotep, Paneb would certainly have the right to some of his property. There is obviously a great deal about the relationship between Paneb and Neferhotep that Amennakhte leaves unsaid.

77 *Stela of Paneb. The foreman Paneb, the object of Amennakhte's attack, worships the goddess Meretseger in the form of a serpent. Below are his sons, including the eldest, Aapahte, who was accused of crimes as an accomplice of his father.*

Amennakhte then proceeds to list a number of charges against Paneb, some of them major and some relatively minor:

When the burial of all the kings was made, I reported Paneb's theft of the things of King Seti Merenptah.

Charge concerning his going to the burial of Henutmire [a queen of Ramesses II] and taking away a goose [presumably a model]. He took an oath by the Lord concerning it saying: It is not in my possession, but they found it in his house.

He went down to the tomb of the workman Nakhtmin and stole the bed which was under him. He carried off the objects which one gives to a dead man and stole them.

He took away the spikes of Pharaoh and the hoe for work in his own tomb.
Charge concerning his ordering the workmen to cut down stones on the top of the tomb of Seti Merenptah. They took them away to his tomb and he erected four columns in his tomb of these stones.

109

Charge concerning his ordering the workmen to work on the plaited bed of the deputy of the temple of Amun, while their wives wove clothes for him. He made Nebnufer son of Wadjmose feeder of his ox for two whole months.

Paneb was also accused of having illicit sexual intercourse with the lady Tuy 'while she was the wife to the workman Kenna' and with two other married ladies in the community and the daughter of one of them, who was also enjoyed by his son the deputy Aapahte.

The main charges against Paneb are the following: robbery of royal tombs, robbery of private tombs, misappropriation of government equipment for private use, use of government employees for private work, presumably in government time, and tyrannical behaviour towards members of the community including sexual assaults on their wives. The petition ends with the hint of an even worse crime:

Nay but such conduct is indeed unworthy of this office. Ah, he is keeping well although he is like a mad man. Yet it was he who killed those men that they might not bring a message to Pharaoh. Lo, I have caused the vizier to know about his way of life.

Were the charges true? As the eventual outcome of this petition is unclear, the true extent of Paneb's misdeeds is no longer known. However, the charge of the misuse of government employees for private work can be confirmed from the surviving records of the daily work rota. In year 1 of Siptah (c. 1196 BC) the draughtsman Neferhotep was absent 'painting the coffin of Paneb' on several occasions. In year 2 of Siptah Nebnufer son of Wadjmose was absent for several days 'feeding his ox', thus confirming directly one of the charges against Paneb. Other workmen are recorded as working in his tomb. In fairness to Paneb, these work records also indicate that workmen were absent on tasks for the other foreman Hay, and even the vizier. Obviously the use of these craftsmen by their superiors was one of the perks of the job. Possibly Paneb carried matters to an extreme. Unfortunately, his tomb has not survived, apart from an underground chamber made when he was only a workman, so we cannot judge the extent of the work done when he was foreman. It seems likely that this charge may not have been regarded as seriously as some of the rest.

There is no doubt that a trial was eventually held and Paneb was removed from office. In year 29 of Ramesses III (c. 1158 BC), an otherwise unknown son or descendant of his named Penanuket remarked: 'you have seen the view of the vizier Hori regarding the place from which stones were removed, when it was said to him: The foreman Paneb, my father, had men remove stones from it'. Obviously the charge of illicitly removing stones from the royal tomb had been proved, and this verdict was later used as a precedent. If the other charges were also proved, then surely Paneb would have been executed. He and his son Aapahte disappear abruptly from the records of the community, but as our documentation at the end of the Nineteenth Dynasty and the beginning of the Twentieth Dynasty is relatively sparse it cannot be determined precisely when this happened. It would seem that Amennakhte, who may have initiated the charges against Paneb, did not reap his desired reward. In year 11 of Ramesses III (c. 1176 BC), when the documents start to become abundant again, Paneb's eventual successor is named as Nekhemmut. He was not related directly to the family of Neferhotep, who had held the post before Paneb, but he had been a simple workman during Paneb's term of office and, indeed, his son Khons was named by Amennakhte as one of Paneb's henchmen. Perhaps one day more details of this intriguing episode in the history of the community will be revealed.

The example of Paneb did not apparently put an end to misdeeds on the part of some workmen. In year 29 of Ramesses III (c. 1158 BC) Paneb's son or descendant Penanuket himself accused the workmen Userhat and Pentaweret of robbing stones from the tomb of Ramesses II and stealing an ox which belonged to the mortuary temple of this same king. Another charge, which appears to have been standard in cases of this nature, was the seduction of three married women in the village. These charges seem to have failed to impress the authorities, as Userhat was still in office as a workman some twelve years later. Penanuket also continued to serve as a workman in the community so his charges did not rebound against him.

During the course of the Twentieth Dynasty the control of the central government slackened. Payments to the workers became more erratic. The Theban area was unsettled by attacks of Libyan raiders, and the royal tombs offered a golden opportunity for enrichment for anyone able and willing to plunder them. It would appear that at some time prior to year 9 of Ramesses IX (c. 1117 BC) the tomb of one of his predecessors, Ramesses VI, which had only been sealed about fifteen years earlier, was violated. Apparently another unnamed tomb had been broken into first, and copper and silver objects were removed. The thieves then quarrelled about the division of the spoils, and an informer threatened to tell the authorities unless he too was paid. Therefore the thieves decided to loot the tomb of Ramesses VI to increase their shares: 'I spent four days breaking into it, we being five'. None of the thieves had any apparent connection with the Deir el-Medina community. However, one of the gang did inquire about the whereabouts of a necropolis worker, who had, it seems, been in on the previous job. The ominous answer was that he had been killed. Once inside the tomb, the men removed metal vessels and garments. Unfortunately, the papyrus which records these events is damaged and the whole story is not known, but, as it is a court record, it is obvious that the thieves were caught and punished. In year 9 of Ramesses IX the tomb of Ramesses VI was inspected and doubtless resealed. The pharaohs slumbered on in peace, but not for very much longer.

78　The tomb of Ramesses VI in the Valley of the Kings is in the foreground
opposite the rest-house. The tomb of Tutankhamun, which lies nearby, was
hidden during construction of this later tomb.

Justice

While the Valley of the Kings was guarded more or less adequately, the tombs of the nobles and the royal tombs of the Seventeenth Dynasty, which were cut into the cliff facing the Nile, and the tombs in the Valley of the Queens were much easier targets for any would-be tomb-robber. In the course of the reign of Ramesses IX they became the prey of an organized gang. The police in the area were under the control of the mayor of Thebes-West, Pawero. Either Pawero and the police knew nothing about these depredations, or they failed to take any action. Eventually rumours of these thefts reached the ears of the mayor of Thebes-East, Paser, who openly denounced these activities. As a result a special commission was set up in year 16 of Ramesses IX consisting of the vizier, several royal butlers and several other notables. It is evident from the surviving records that the mayor of Thebes-West and his staff, including the workmen of the necropolis, were not amused by the implied criticism of their competence in guarding the royal tombs and tried their best to ensure a whitewash. Ten royal tombs were examined by the commission, none of which was in the Valley of the Kings, but only one, that of King Sobekemsaf of the Seventeenth Dynasty, was found to have been violated by thieves who had tunnelled through from a neighbouring private tomb: 'The burial chamber of the king was found empty of its lord and likewise the burial chamber of the great royal wife Nubkhas, his wife, the robbers having laid hands upon them'. The commission then proceeded to examine the private tombs which lay in the cliffs on the west bank:

It was found that the thieves had robbed them all, dragging their owners out from their inner coffins and outer coffins . . . and stealing their funerary equipment which had been given to them with the gold, silver, and the fittings which were in their inner coffins.

A list of suspected thieves was placed before the commission and they were arrested pending investigation. The commission moved on to the Valley of the Queens taking with it a confessed thief who claimed to have robbed the tomb of Queen Isis, wife of Ramesses III. He failed to identify the correct tomb and, without detailed investigations, the commission declared that the tombs in the valley were intact. The inhabitants of the west bank, notably the police and royal workmen, took the findings of the commission as a complete vindication of themselves and launched a noisy demonstration aimed principally against the mayor of Thebes-East, Paser. A violent altercation ensued between Paser and Userkhepesh, the foreman at Deir el-Medina:

The mayor of Thebes said to the people of the necropolis: You have rejoiced over me at the very door of my house. What do you mean by it? . . . If you are rejoicing about the tomb in which you have been and examined and found intact, yet . . . Sobekemsaf has been robbed together with Nubkhas his royal wife.

The chief workman Userkhepesh replied:

All the kings with their royal wives and royal mothers and royal children who rest in the great and noble necropolis together with those who rest in the Place of Beauty [Valley of the Queens] are intact. They are protected and ensured for eternity. The wise counsel of Pharaoh their child guards and examines them strictly.

This last statement was a bare-faced lie, as Userkhepesh calmly overlooked the fate of Sobekemsaf and all the private tombs on the west bank. Unable to contain his anger and indignation any longer Paser blurted out:

The scribe Harshire son of Amennakhte of the Tomb . . . and the scribe Pabasa of the Tomb have told me five very serious capital charges against you. I am writing about them to Pharaoh my lord in order that servants of Pharaoh may be sent to deal with all of you.

This retort took place in the presence of the mayor of Thebes-West, Pawero, who immediately complained to the vizier:

It was an offence on the part of those two scribes of the Tomb that they should go to the mayor of Thebes to report to him whereas their predecessors never reported to him but they reported to the vizier . . .

In other words, the scribes were guilty of administrative error in not reporting through the proper channels and should be reprimanded. The next day the royal commission sat and found these new charges baseless. It may be that Paser, in an excess of zeal possibly inspired by political

79 *The Abbott Papyrus. This papyrus forms part of the record of the activities of a royal commission which was investigating the robberies of the royal tombs in the reign of Ramesses IX.*

reasons as well as concern for the dead pharaohs, had come up with un-substantiated charges, but Pawero's actions could hardly be termed disinterested.

Meanwhile, the interrogation of the suspected thieves was taking place. The authorities were not too gentle with those believed to have violated the tomb of King Sobekemsaf. The chief suspect Amenpanufer was interrogated with a stick until he confessed. A similar method of interrogation by which the culprit was beaten on the soles of the feet, known as the bastinado, was in use in Egypt in the nineteenth century. Amenpanufer confessed that he and seven others had robbed the tomb of Sobekemsaf:

We opened their outer coffins and their inner coffins in which they lay. We found the noble mummy of this king equipped with a sword. A large number of amulets and ornaments of gold were upon his neck. His mask of gold was upon him. The noble mummy of the king was completely covered with gold. His coffins were adorned with gold and silver inside and out and inlaid with all kinds of precious stones. We collected the gold which we found on this noble mummy of this god and on his amulets and jewels which were upon his neck and on the coffins in which he lay. We found the queen in exactly the same state and we collected all that we found on her likewise. We set fire to their coffins. We stole their furniture that we found with them consisting of articles of gold, silver, and bronze and divided them up amongst ourselves.

The coffins were burnt in order to extract the jewels and precious metal more easily from the wooden surrounds.

Amenpanufer was unlucky. Rumour of his theft soon reached the authorities and he was arrested. However, he managed to bribe the local official to release him. On his return his partners made good his loss. He then embarked on a new spree of tomb-robbery until his recent arrest led to his confession. It is noteworthy that none of the eight thieves were attached to the Deir el-Medina community but were employed by various temples in the Theban area. A further seventeen culprits were identified as looters of private tombs. The list is not complete but, again, only one of the men appears to have been employed by the necropolis authorities and may not have been resident in the village. Those convicted of tomb-robbery were put to death; the method of their execution is not known but probably involved mutilation and impaling. It made a great enough impression to be remembered by a suspected thief about thirty years later: 'I saw the punishment which was inflicted on the thieves in the time of the vizier Khaemwese. Is it then likely that I should seek such a death?'

Thus it would seem that in year 16 of Ramesses IX the workmen's community had emerged nearly unscathed from the accusations of tomb-robbery which were circulating in the Theban area. Pawero had managed to discomfit, if not to discredit, his fellow-mayor Paser and play down the activities of those who were nominally under his control. However, events in that year showed that the community of Deir el-Medina was divided. The assurances of the foreman Userkhepesh were not matched by the denunciations of the scribes of the Tomb in the same village. The events of the following year are obscure. It appears that investigations by the commission were not suspended, and more evidence was found to implicate several senior members of the community. Eight workmen were arrested, including the two deputies. Quantities of stolen goods were recovered from the homes of the accused and various members of the west-bank settlements who were named as receivers of stolen goods. A new tour of inspection showed that the tomb of Queen Isis had indeed been robbed as had been reported in the previous year. The arrests seem to have led to a purge of the administration of the village. The foremen including the argumentative Userkhepesh disappear. They had inherited their positions from their fathers and grandfathers. The new appointments of foremen and deputies were made directly from the ranks of the ordinary workmen. The scribes who had reported the thefts naturally retained their offices. Pawero also seems to have managed to stay in office and is still recorded about thirty years later. There are no further records of what became of Paser.

Information on the community and western Thebes in the next few years is scanty. Civil war ravaged the Theban area at least twice in a decade. The village of Deir el-Medina was abandoned and its inhabitants sought refuge behind the walls of the mortuary temple of Ramesses III at Medinet Habu. Even here safety was not guaranteed: the temple was stormed by unruly troops, its treasures looted, and several refugees enslaved. In such circumstances the Valley of the Kings was a tempting target. It seems likely that the royal tombs were looted and desecrated during one of these disturbances, possibly during the second outbreak about year 18 of Ramesses XI (c. 1081 BC), when the royal treasures were stolen and the bodies were stripped of their jewellery, and sometimes even ripped apart in the search for wealth. It seems unlikely that members of the community were directly involved in this wholesale assault on the royal valley. They could hardly compete with the soldiery in the area. However, there can be no doubt that some of them, and other residents of the west bank, took advantage of the chaos of the time to loot less accessible tombs in the Valley of the Queens and help themselves to temple treasures.

In year 19 of Ramesses XI order was finally restored in the Theban area. An attempt was made to recover stolen property and punish some of the thieves still left in the vicinity. Thirteen men were identified as having robbed the tombs of queens, but only one of them was a workman of the community, although he did play a key role, since he pointed out to the robbers the tomb of one of the queens. He is stated to have claimed only a small share of the loot 'so my fellow necropolis-workers will not denounce me'. This would imply that most of the other workmen were still honest. It is likely that only a small percentage of goods were recovered from the thieves. Most of the surviving records deal with robbery from temples rather than tombs and the workmen of the community were not involved in these. The royal mummies and the remains of their funerary equipment were gathered together by the surviving workers and reburied in two secret caches after repairs had been made to the bodies. The great tomb-robberies marked the end of the activities of the community, since after Ramesses XI there were to be no more royal tombs at Thebes.

80 (above) *The house of the scribe Butehamun, at Medinet Habu; only two rooms have been preserved.*

81 (below) *The temple of Medinet Habu. This mortuary temple was built by Ramesses III and decorated with scenes of his victories, notably over the Sea-Peoples. In the later part of the Twentieth Dynasty it served as a refuge for the community from Deir el-Medina.*

7 Deir el-Medina Rediscovered

THE VILLAGE OF Deir el-Medina was deserted by its inhabitants some time during the reign of Ramesses XI (c. 1098–1069 BC). The increasing Libyan raids and civil wars made the Theban area unsafe and the workmen moved to the protection of the mortuary temple of Ramesses III at Medinet Habu, although even there safety was not assured. The scribe Butehamun built for himself a spacious home in the temple precincts. Only two main rooms have been preserved, one with four columns and the other with one pair. It is probably on this site, or another nearby, that his father Dhutmose's house was situated, as lintels which have been recovered suggest. The scribes Dhutmose and Butehamun came from a scribal family which had held office at Deir el-Medina since the appointment of Amennakhte son of Ipuy in year 16 of Ramesses III (c. 1171 BC), and they continued to play an important role during the last years of the community. Dhutmose's private correspondence has survived, and through his letters it is possible to follow the community's disintegration. It seems that work at first proceeded normally on the tomb of Ramesses XI, despite the move to Medinet Habu, although lists of the workmen in years 8 and 9 appear smaller than usual. Dhutmose had to make a special journey south of Thebes to extort the payment of taxes in kind to feed the community.

The military situation in Thebes and the subsequent civil war in Nubia led to a drain on manpower. Many workmen were conscripted or chose to abandon their posts for fear of conscription. Dhutmose wrote at one point:

We are living here in Medinet Habu . . . However, the boys of the Tomb have gone. They are living in Thebes, while I am living here alone with the scribe of the army Pentahunakhte. Please have the men of the Tomb who are there in Thebes assembled and send them to me to this side [of the river] . . . Put them under the supervision of the scribe Butehamun.

Dhutmose himself was soon ordered to join the Nubian campaign against the rebel Panehsi. He sent back a steady stream of letters to his son Butehamun, who had been left in charge in Thebes. Dhutmose appears to

82 *Letter of the scribe Butehamun, to the High Priest of Amun and general Paiankh, who was on campaign in Nubia. It assured him that certain orders, which he had given, had been carried out by the workmen.*

have brought supplies to the royal army, but he fell ill on his journey south. His subsequent fate is unclear, but his son Butehamun later prays for a ripe old age that was denied to his father. Dhutmose died about year 28 of Ramesses XI (*c.* 1071 BC), and his royal master shortly afterwards. The tomb of Ramesses XI was the last royal tomb to be built in the Valley of the Kings, but there is no evidence that the king was actually buried there. He was succeeded by Smendes, first ruler of the Twenty-first Dynasty, whose capital was at Tanis in the Delta and it is here that he and his successors were buried. There were to be no more royal burials at Thebes, and the worker's community at Deir el-Medina ceased to have a reason to exist.

The bulk of the work-force must have disappeared by the early Twenty-first Dynasty, either through conscription, flight to avoid this fate, or disbandment. The officers of the community, the two foremen and the scribes, carried on with whatever workmen remained. Their role was not now to prepare the tombs of living rulers, but rather to repair and preserve the ravaged burials of the previous monarchs. Following the civil wars in the Theban area, the tombs in the Valley of the Kings lay open and empty. The bodies of the former rulers and their relations were gathered together on the orders of high priests of Amun, who were now the virtual rulers of the Theban area, and were secretly reburied with what little possessions remained. Butehamun and his sons aided in this pious task. The bodies were hidden in two separate caches. From time to time one cache, near Deir el-Bahri, was opened to admit the bodies of the high priests of Thebes and their relations: in year 10 of Siamun two foremen of Deir el-Medina are named as taking part in such a ceremony. Thereafter the royal cache was sealed and the royal mummies and their necropolis workmen forgotten until excavations in the nineteenth century brought them to light once more.

Even after it was abandoned the village of Deir el-Medina was still visited by its former inhabitants. The temples were presumably frequented during the day when conditions permitted, and the empty houses were used as places of storage. The family papers of the scribe Dhutmose were placed for safe-keeping in the house of his grandfather, but unfortunately they were soaked in a rainstorm. They were rescued and stored in his great-grandfather's tomb, the roof of which was doubtless in better preservation. During the Twenty-first and Twenty-second Dynasties the village must have fallen into disuse. Although the deserted cemetery was presumably plundered and several tombs were taken over for reuse, there is no evidence that any of the individuals buried in the valley in this period were in any way connected with the original inhabitants.

In the Ptolemaic period the valley was reinvigorated by the construction of a temple dedicated to Hathor and Maat by Ptolemy IV (222–205 BC). It was built on the site of earlier temples which had served Deir el-Medina, but it is not known whether these temples had continued to function until the Ptolemaic period. The work of construction was continued and expanded under the successors of Ptolemy IV, and the complex was finally completed in the Roman period. A large cache of demotic papyri dating from 188 to 101 BC has been found near the temple, where it had been hidden in two jars. The documents reflect the life of the priests who served the temple and probably lived in the vicinity of Medinet Habu. The papyri consist of property sales, marriage contracts and deeds of divorce. The temple was possibly visited by the many Greek, and later Roman, tourists who journeyed up the Nile to see the wonders of the pharaohs. The Valley of the Kings and its deserted tombs were a prominent feature of any tour, along with the other sites on the west bank. Few probably suspected that the homes of the men who built the tombs lay buried near the Ptolemaic temple of Deir el-Medina.

At some time during this period two deep New Kingdom shafts in the north of the valley were reused for later burials. In one shaft the black schist coffin of the priestess Ankhnesneferibre, daughter of Psamtik II, who died in 525 BC or later, was installed together with assorted building blocks which came originally from a temple of King Taharqa of the Twenty-fifth Dynasty (690–664 BC). This was not the original burial of the princess which has since been located at Medinet Habu. Her coffin had been reinscribed in places for the prophet of Monthu Pimonthu. He must have removed her coffin from Medinet Habu, although he could hardly have accomplished this task single-handed. Presumably he removed the Taharqa blocks from some other site, so their existence does not necessarily mean that a temple of this king stood in the valley of Deir el-Medina. Possibly other remains of the Twenty-sixth Dynasty which have been found in the valley were brought there from Medinet Habu at this time. In a neighbouring shaft the pink granite

83 *The Ptolemaic temple at Deir el-Medina. The temple, its gateway and side buildings bear the names of a number of Graeco-Roman rulers including Ptolemies IV, VI, VII, IX and XII and Augustus Caesar.*

84 *Ptolemaic relief. On the right Ptolemy IX makes an offering to Hathor, who carries the young Horus, and Maat; on the left he appears with his mother Cleopatra III.*

85 *The sarcophagus lid of Ankhnesneferibre. This daughter of Psamtik II became high priestess of Amun at Thebes in 584 BC in succession to her great-aunt, who had adopted her in 595 BC. Our last record of her is in 525 BC, the year of the Persian conquest of Egypt. It is not known if she was ever laid to rest in her splendid. sarcophagus.*

sarcophagus of Nitocris, a predecessor of Ankhnesneferibre, was placed. It, too, was probably brought from Medinet Habu and reused in a Ptolemaic burial. In the basement of one of the houses in the village of Deir el-Medina a burial of the Roman period has been discovered, consisting of five rectangular wooden coffins, one anthropoid wooden coffin and ten mummies, two of which were not in the coffins. With the coming of Christianity the temple of Hathor was converted into a church and a monastery arose on the site, probably dedicated to St Isidorus the Martyr. The Coptic buildings and burials mark the final use of the Deir el-Medina valley prior to its abandonment to total desolation in the eighth or ninth century AD. However, the occupation of the monks gave the area its Arabic name of Deir el-Medina, 'the monastery of the town'. As the sands covered it, only the Ptolemaic temple remained visible to the infrequent travellers who passed by.

At the beginning of the eighteenth century Thebes, now the Arabic village of Luxor, was rediscovered for European scholars by that intrepid traveller and preacher Père Claude Sicard (1677–1726). However, the political state of the country of Egypt was too unstable to allow any but the most determined to venture into the depths of the countryside where law and order was only lightly maintained. In January 1738 Richard Pococke (1704–65) reached Thebes on his way to Aswan. He toured the west bank and saw the tombs in the Valley of the Kings. He does not describe the valley of Deir el-Medina but among the plans he drew there is one of the Ptolemaic temple, which means that he obviously visited the valley. Other travellers in the eighteenth century have left only brief accounts and do not mention Deir el-Medina. The political situation in Egypt changed dramatically in 1798, when Napoleon Bonaparte invaded the country as part of the French revolutionary government's war against Britain and her allies. The French were well aware of Egypt's potential as a repository of ancient monuments. A special team of French scholars accompanied the army to report on the country, its resources and its antiquities. The engineers Prosper Jollois (1776–1842) and René Devilliers (1780–1855) reached Luxor in late June 1799 on the way south to Aswan, and returned briefly in July to catalogue the monuments on the west bank of the Nile. These included the Ptolemaic temple at Deir el-Medina, mistakenly termed a temple of Isis. The other ruins on this site are not mentioned and were presumably still hidden beneath the sand.

In 1777 the first identifiable object from Deir el-Medina made its appearance. A statuette of the workman Neferabu, who flourished early in the reign of Ramesses II (c. 1279–1212 BC), was acquired in the Theban region by an Italian monk, who was doubtless in Egypt in search of converts from the Coptic community. He brought the object to Cairo where it was given to Baron François de Tott (1730–93), who had arrived on a diplomatic mission for the King of France. It was seen and drawn by

86, 87 *Statue of Neferabu. On the left is an engraving of the drawing published by Sonnini de Manoncour in 1799, and on the right the original statue, now in Malta. Part of the base has been damaged but can be restored from the earlier drawing.*

Tott's companion the naturalist Charles Sonnini de Manoncour (1751–1812), although his account was not published until 1799, by which time the statue had disappeared from view. In the middle of the nineteenth century it reappeared somewhat more damaged in Malta and now resides in the Valetta Museum. An account published in 1882 assured readers that it had been discovered on the island of Gozo in 1713, but, thanks to Sonnini's description, it can be confirmed that it did not leave Egypt until the second half of the eighteenth century.

The Napoleonic invasion was a military and political failure. The French army was eventually forced to surrender to the combined British and Turkish forces. The antiquities which the French scholars had collected were confiscated by the victors. The objects, including the famous Rosetta Stone, were sent to London and now adorn the galleries of the British Museum. During the brief British presence in Egypt William Hamilton (1777–1859) had visited Thebes from December 1801 – January 1802. He describes the Ptolemaic temple of Deir el-Medina but, again, no other ruins. The French invasion, however, did have one important consequence. The Egyptian political scene was totally disrupted, enabling the ambitious and competent Muhammad Ali (1769–1849), an Albanian in Turkish service, to install himself as Pasha of Egypt. He provided the country with a strong central government which could ensure the safety of travellers within its borders. The arrival of the Egyptian antiquities in London and the publications of the returned French scholars awakened great interest in Egypt and its past among the Europeans. The wars which engulfed that continent until 1815 prevented much travel, apart from military and diplomatic missions. Following Waterloo, and with peace in Europe, Egypt suddenly became the destination of travellers and scholars alike.

Bernardino Drovetti (1776–1852), Italian-born French consul in Egypt, foresaw the growing European interest in Egyptian antiquities and the profits that it might yield. As early as 1811 he had begun to excavate in Thebes in order to amass a private collection with the intention of disposing of it in due course to a European museum. In 1814 he was dismissed from office for Napoleonic sympathies, but he remained in Egypt and was able to devote more time to exploration and the search for antiquities. Such was his influence with Muhammad Ali that the French government reappointed him to his old office in 1821. Apart from periodic visits, he did not personally oversee the excavations but employed agents to acquire most of the objects in his collection. His most important agents were the Italian Antonio Lebolo and the Frenchmen Joseph Rosignani and Jean Jacques Rifaud (1786–1852). They employed native workmen to dig under their supervision, but they also relied heavily on the locals bringing objects to them without questioning where these might have been found. Indeed, the knowledge that these crazy Europeans were willing to pay for ancient relics sparked off a renewal of the old Egyptian profession of tomb-robbery.

The importance of the valley of Deir el-Medina as a source of antiquities was known as early as 1815. In that year Sven Lidman (1784–1845), a Swede attached to his country's embassy at Istanbul, and Otto Friedrich von Richter (1792–1816), a Baltic nobleman who acted as Lidman's secretary, passed through Luxor on their way to and from Nubia. Both men took the opportunity to form small collections of antiquities. That of Richter certainly contained Deir el-Medina stelae, while it is probable that at least one such stela found its way into Lidman's hands. The French team in Luxor, which was to acquire an unpleasant reputation for its possessive attitude towards its excavation sites, is unlikely to have tolerated any intrusion, and so it can be safely assumed that in 1815 Drovetti's team was not encamped in Deir el-Medina and that the antiquities supplied to Lidman and Richter were bought from natives working the area on a free-lance basis. Many of the Deir el-Medina pieces in Drovetti's collection presumably came from these same independent

Deir el-Medina Rediscovered

sources. Unfortunately, neither Lidman nor Richter published a full account of their travels in Egypt, although Lidman's notebooks still survive. Lidman's collection was destroyed in a fire in Istanbul in 1818. One Deir el-Medina stela apparently survived or was disposed of before the fire and is now in the museum at Uppsala, Sweden. On Richter's premature death in 1816 his papers and antiquities were sent to his parents in Estonia. His father presented the objects to the University Museum of Dorpat (Tartu) where they were seen and published at the end of last century. They were then lost to view and were presumed to have perished in the convulsions which swept this part of the world in the first half of the twentieth century. It now transpires that they were moved to Voronezh for safety in the First World War and are now preserved in the Museum of Fine Arts in that town. In 1815 the British traveller William Bankes (1787–1855) also passed through Luxor, but it is not certain whether he acquired his collection of Deir el-Medina stelae at this time or on his second visit in 1818. Thus the site of the community of Deir el-Medina was discovered between 1811 and 1815 and was to be exploited with vigour for the next few years.

In the spring of 1815 Henry Salt (1780–1827) was appointed British consul in Egypt through the influence of his patron George Annesley, Viscount Valentia (1770–1844), for whom he had acted as secretary on an earlier trip to India and Ethiopia. Salt's candidacy was also supported by Charles Yorke (1764–1834), a noted antiquarian and politician, and Sir Joseph Banks (1743–1820), a Trustee of the British Museum. Prior to his departure Valentia asked Salt to procure for him some Egyptian antiquities. Banks also intimated that the British Museum would welcome any effort to increase its Egyptian collection. Salt arrived in Egypt in March 1816 and by December he could write to his patron Valentia:

For some time after my arrival owing to plague I met with no antiquities which are becoming difficult to purchase and I found that Monsieur Drovetti the quondam French consul was in Upper Egypt buying up everything there to complete a collection upon which he has been engaged some years . . .

Since our release from quarantine I have taken every possible means to collect and am glad to say that I have been very successful so that I shall in the spring have to send you a cargo of such things as I believe you have not before seen. I must however inform you that I am so bit with the prospect of what may still be done in Upper Egypt, as to feel unable to abstain from forming a collection myself; you may however depend upon coming in for a good share . . .

Unfortunately, the first shipment of antiquities to Lord Valentia was severely damaged in transit.

In the spring of 1816 Salt was introduced to Giovanni Belzoni (1778–1823), a one-time circus strongman in London, who had come to Egypt to seek his fortune. Luck had not favoured him and he was now unemployed. Belzoni offered to arrange transport of a large head of Ramesses

88 *Stela of Didi. This came from the private collection of Belzoni and must have been acquired by him from natives during his stay at Luxor.*

11, known as the 'Young Memnon', from its temple at Thebes down to Cairo. Salt agreed to pay his expenses and asked him to collect other antiquities on the journey. Belzoni set off with his wife, an Irishwoman, who was the first European woman to penetrate Upper Egypt. His trip was very successful. The head was at once dispatched as a gift to the British Museum, while the other antiquities were secured by Salt for his new collection. Salt immediately sent Belzoni back to Thebes with his secretary Henry Beechey (c. 1790–c. 1860) and his interpreter Giovanni d'Athanasi (1799–c. 1850) to acquire more objects. The appearance of the British team was not well received by the agents of the French consul. Relations between the two groups, both largely composed of Italians, were frigid. Belzoni was once physically threatened by his rivals. Belzoni

Deir el-Medina Rediscovered

and some of his successors solved the problem of accommodation in this remote area by following the local Arab custom of moving into an old tomb. Neither party left accurate details as to where their excavations were conducted, but from Belzoni's account it is known that he dug in the temple of Karnak on the east bank and by the colossi of Memnon and in the Valley of the Kings on the west bank. Drovetti's team is known to have excavated at Karnak and at tombs in Gurna on the west bank. As both the Salt and Drovetti collections contained Deir el-Medina material, it seems probable that most of these were acquired via native middlemen rather than through direct excavations.

In November 1817 Henry Salt arrived in Luxor to see the ruins for himself and to check on the progress of his excavations. He accompanied a tourist party headed by Somerset Lowry-Corry, second Earl of Belmore (1774–1841), his wife, sons, brother, chaplain and private physician Dr R. Richardson (1779–1847), who wrote an account of the journey. The tourists proceeded to Nubia, but Belmore commissioned Giovanni d'Athanasi, in his absence, to acquire antiquities for his own private collection. On his return to Thebes in January 1818 these were shown to Belmore and included 'stones covered with deities, offerings, priests, and hieroglyphics: all of which were sufficiently curious and interesting'. Further antiquities were collected during a stay in the Theban area in January and February. These antiquities included a large number of stelae from Deir el-Medina made by the royal workmen for their own use. A missing corner from one of the stelae was to be discovered in excavations ninety years later. The party also visited the site of Deir el-Medina, but Richardson only mentions the Ptolemaic temple and the 'burial ground of the former Christian possessors whose sepulchres the Arabs are now ransacking for antiquities'. He thought that the temple was 'the most entire and most highly finished of all the temples in Thebes'.

In February the party set off back to Cairo carrying Lord Belmore's antiquities, a portion of Salt's collection and probably some more, including Deir el-Medina stelae, which were destined for Salt's patron Viscount Valentia, now Earl of Mountnorris. Like the previous shipment to Valentia, Belmore's antiquities had a rough passage to Britain and several papyri were needlessly destroyed. Belmore was later to publish selections from his collection in a sumptuous and highly accurate edition. The Frenchman Rifaud also attempted to publish some of his acquisitions, including Deir el-Medina pieces, but his copies of hieroglyphs are unintelligible. While in Luxor, Belmore and his party met the French traveller Frédéric Cailliaud (1787–1869), who was in the Theban area in 1816 and again in 1817, 1818, 1820 and 1822, at which times he conducted his own excavations for antiquities. He is not too precise as to the locations, but he may possibly have entered one of the tombs at Deir el-Medina. The Swedish consul in Egypt, most confusingly named Giovanni Anastasi (1780–

1857), also decided to join in the hunt for antiquities, and amassed a collection with the help of yet another Italian named Piccinini, who operated in the Theban area.

The dispersal of the great collections began almost as soon as their formation. It had always been Salt's intention to offer his antiquities to the British Museum in return for payment of his considerable expenses. He was horrified to discover that the Museum was now having second thoughts about increasing its Egyptian holdings. By 1821 the whole of the collection had been forwarded to London, and after several years of haggling was purchased by the Trustees of the British Museum in 1823, with the exception of the celebrated sarcophagus of Seti I, which was later bought by Sir John Soane for his own museum. Among the pieces in the Salt collection was the petition against the foreman Paneb which has already been mentioned (p. 107). His experience with the authorities of the British Museum so depressed Salt that his second collection formed from 1819 to 1824 was sold directly to the French government, who, as a result of Napoleon's adventures, were more interested and more willing to pay for Egyptian antiquities. A third collection which included Deir el-Medina pieces was completed just prior to Salt's death and was

89 *The collection of the Earl of Belmore. This drawing shows the manner in which the Egyptian collection was displayed in the Earl's home. Quite a number of pieces, now in the British Museum, can be identified from this sketch.*

eventually sold in London in 1835, when the British Museum acquired more material. Salt's agent d'Athanasi continued to excavate on his own initiative and sold two collections in London in 1837 and 1845 from which more Deir el-Medina objects entered the British Museum. The Museum's holdings were further enriched by the purchase of the Belmore collection in 1843 and the donation of some objects from the Valentia collection in 1854. The Bankes collection remains the sole survivor of these early British collections still in private hands.

Drovetti also had difficulties in disposing of his collection. He first offered it to France, but his terms were too high and his offer was refused. It was eventually sold to the King of Sardinia in 1824 and is now housed in the Museo Egizio, Turin. A large part of this collection consisted of items from Deir el-Medina, including some very fine stone and wooden statues of the workmen and their gods, a large number of stelae and, most important of all, numerous papyrus fragments. Many of the papyri had been found incomplete, but others may have been broken as a result of the journey from Thebes to Cairo and thence to Italy. Work still continues on piecing the various documents together. These consist of literary texts, census lists, attendance registers, and possibly the famous erotic papyrus which probably came from Deir el-Medina. With this collection Turin acquired the most famous of Egyptian papyri – the Canon of Kings, a list of every recognized Egyptian ruler from the beginning of time until the age of the Ramessides. If it had been preserved intact, how much easier the study of Egyptian history would be. It is unlikely that such a document originated from the workmen's village, but certainly there were scribes such as Kenherkhepeshef who would have prized it. The collection of the Swedish consul Anastasi was purchased by the Museum of Leiden in 1828. Various other museums, and those already named, received Deir el-Medina material which escaped the major collections and filtered back to Europe through various channels. The Danish consul in Egypt sent some stelae to the National Museum in Copenhagen in 1821. A stela has recently been identified in a museum at Bordeaux. It is likely that some items have escaped the eyes of Egyptologists and still lie hidden in some minor museum or private collection.

The initial burst of activity appears to have exhausted the rich vein of material at Deir el-Medina, and the collectors turned elsewhere. The era of the amateur was now ending and that of the scholar was about to begin. The decipherment of hieroglyphs by Jean François Champollion (1790–1832) was now opening the door to the understanding of Egyptian history. One of the new breed of scholars was John Gardner Wilkinson (1797–1875), later knighted, who went to Egypt in 1821 and stayed there for twelve years recording monuments. While in Thebes in 1827 and 1828, he undertook the excavation of a number of tombs at Deir el-Medina and so made them accessible for the first time. About the same time Robert Hay

90 *A Hay Manuscript. This is a drawing of the tomb of the workman Pashed.
The sarcophagus in the centre was broken up after Hay's visit, and copies of its
inscriptions survive only in his manuscripts.*

(1799–1863) with a team of artists and draughtsmen, was also at work. He
himself copied one recently discovered tomb at Deir el-Medina in 1834.
Wilkinson and Hay also copied the inscriptions on a number of objects
belonging to the workmen of Deir el-Medina which were in circulation in
the Theban area but have now vanished. Their work remains largely
unpublished to this day. In 1828–29 the celebrated Champollion visited
Egypt and himself made copies of some of the Deir el-Medina tombs.

In 1831 the French government sent a naval expedition to Egypt to
remove from Luxor an obelisk which had been offered to France by the
Pasha. While the crew were waiting for the Nile to flood so they could
transport their prize down the river, they decided to explore the area for
antiquities. On the advice of Rosignani, Drovetti's former assistant, they
turned their attention to Deir el-Medina. On 28 February 1832 they

managed to raise a large black schist sarcophagus from a deep pit in the
north of the valley. It was the coffin of the priestess Ankhnesneferibre. The
sailors left some papers in the pit which were retrieved by another French
expedition ninety-six years later. Both obelisk and sarcophagus were
transported back to Paris, and the obelisk was erected in the Place de la
Concorde. The French government, however, showed a distinct lack of
interest in purchasing the sarcophagus from its naval owners, who had to
look elsewhere for a buyer. One did not immediately come forward.

In February 1835 the Trustees of the British Museum considered buying
the sarcophagus but eventually declined to pay the high price which was
demanded. The matter was discussed again at intervals until August of
that year, but nothing further was accomplished. In April 1836 the
Trustees were galvanized into action by a letter from one of their number,
Alexander, Duke of Hamilton (1767–1852), then in Paris. He wrote that he
had seen a magnificent sarcophagus on sale in Paris and could acquire it for
the Museum at a reasonable price. The terms were soon agreed upon and
the Trustees dispatched their cheque to Paris. The Ankhnesneferibre
sarcophagus was theirs. The large crate containing the prize arrived in the
Museum in September 1836 and was opened by the eager staff. They were
aghast to discover that it was not the Ankhnesneferibre sarcophagus but a
green schist anthropoid coffin. 'The Duke has been humbugged by those
rascally Frenchmen'. In reply to an agitated letter, the Duke of Hamilton
declared that, of course it was not the Ankhnesneferibre coffin; he had
never said that it was. If the other Trustees felt that they had been misled,
he would willingly pay the expenses out of his own pocket and keep the
coffin himself. The Trustees agreed to this proposal with alacrity. A
second emissary was sent to Paris to purchase the right sarcophagus. This
time all went well: the Ankhnesneferibre sarcophagus reached the British
Museum in January 1837 and remains one of its prize possessions. As he

91 *The sarcophagus purchased by the Duke of Hamilton.*
The dissimilarity between this sarcophagus and the coffin
of Ankhnesneferibeore (85) is quite evident.

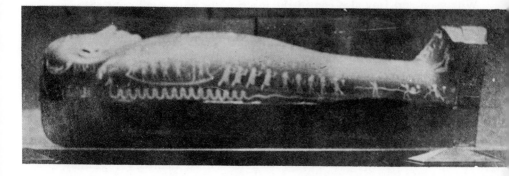

was now the unexpected owner of an Egyptian sarcophagus, the Duke of Hamilton decided that he might as well make use of it. On his death in 1852, he was embalmed according to the Egyptian manner and laid to rest in his Egyptian coffin in his private chapel. Unfortunately, in the 1920s the sarcophagus was removed from the chapel, which was in danger of collapse, and buried in a local cemetery. It is hoped that this Egyptian relic may one day be retrieved from Scottish soil and again be on view to scholars and the general public.

In 1842 Richard Lepsius (1810–84) set off for Egypt at the head of a Prussian expedition to record in detail the monuments of Egypt and to collect objects for the Berlin Museum. On the west bank of the Nile at Thebes in late 1844 the party installed themselves in Wilkinson's old house and set to work copying the tombs, including those at Deir el-Medina. They even succeeded in uncovering some new ones. The opened tombs had deteriorated somewhat since Wilkinson had copied them and some scenes were removed for transport to the safety of the Berlin Museum. Indeed, after the departure of the expedition, some of the tombs were vandalized and scenes were removed for sale to collectors. In 1848 the British Museum purchased a fragment of wall relief in London. With the help of Lepsius's copy, it can be identified as coming from the tomb of the foreman Anherkhau at Deir el-Medina. Comparison reveals that the copy is neither exact nor complete.

In the late 1840s or early 1850s a sensational discovery of papyri was made near either Medinet Habu or Deir el-Medina by native diggers. According to their custom, they divided the spoil among themselves even to the extent of tearing papyri in half. It is impossible to reconstitute the original archive completely, but it undoubtedly included all the tomb-robbery papyri as well as other official documents which were once stored in the archives of the mortuary temple of Ramesses III at Medinet Habu. Several sheets were purchased by the British Museum in 1856 and 1857. Others acquired in Egypt in 1854 or 1855 entered the Mayer collection now at the Merseyside County Museum, Liverpool. Several were acquired by the collector Anthony Harris (1790–1869), whose daughter Selima sold them to the British Museum. Half of one papyrus entered the collection of William Tyssen-Amherst, First Baron Amherst of Hackney (1835–1909), and was later purchased by the Pierpont Morgan Library in New York. In 1935 Jean Capart (1877–1947), curator of the Egyptian collection at Brussels, was invited to examine a small group of antiquities acquired by the future Leopold II on trips to Egypt in 1854 and 1862. While considering a wooden funerary figure, he automatically checked to see whether there might be a funerary papyrus in the hollow cavity. Sure enough a papyrus was present. Later in the day he set about unrolling it. Imagine his astonishment when, instead of the usual religious text, it turned out to be the missing half of the Amherst papyrus. The original or subsequent

92 (above) *An inscription from the tomb of Anherkhau, now in the British Museum.*
93 (below) *Copy by Lepsius of the original inscription from the tomb of Anherkhau.*
Lepsius omitted the last two columns and confused the placing of some of the signs in
the other columns.

94 *Statue of the royal scribe Khay. This hollow wooden figure contained the missing half of the Amherst papyrus which had doubtless been placed there by a native dealer in order to increase the sale price of the unrelated statue.*

native owner of that fragment had tried to maximize its value by placing it in an empty wooden figure and selling that as an intact find with original papyrus. At some stage it was forgotten that the papyrus was there and so it lay undetected until 1935. Fragments of this discovery may yet remain to be unearthed.

Egypt in the latter part of the nineteenth century became a favourite destination for tourists. Many went because the dry climate was considered beneficial for their health, while others were drawn by the lure of the East. The Valley of the Kings and the other monuments on the west bank of the Nile, including the Ptolemaic temple at Deir el-Medina, were viewed by an ever increasing throng of Europeans and Americans. In 1869 one of the most distinguished visitors arrived at Alexandria. The Prince of Wales, the future Edward VII, accompanied by his wife and a large suite, was on an extensive tour of the Middle East. The party sailed up the Nile to Luxor from where they toured the ruins on the west bank on the 17 and 18 February. The Prince and his party then sailed on to the second cataract, but before his departure he instructed the British consul, who remained behind, to undertake excavations on his behalf. Presumably the consul conferred with the British consular agent in Luxor, an Egyptian Mustapha Agha, who also acted as an antiquities dealer. On the return of the Prince in March, he was informed that a significant discovery had been made. Thirty or so coffins had been unearthed from a deep pit on the west bank. On 11 March the royal party hurried across the river to inspect the site of the discovery. A lady-in-waiting to the princess recalled:

Arrived at the spot we could only see a deep entrance cut in the rock. A few people went down, as it were down a coal-pit, by hanging on a rope. Down below I was told there was a magnificent stone sarcophagus said to be that of the beautiful Queen Nitocris which the Prince means to take to England.

The sarcophagus, which according to another account was made of red granite, resisted efforts to remove it. In fact, it was only in 1885 that it was brought to the surface and is now housed in the Cairo Museum. The shaft from which it came can be located in the valley of Deir el-Medina, close to the spot where the French discovered the coffin of Ankhnesneferibre in 1832. However, it is quite probable that the coffin of Nitocris may have been the sole occupant of that shaft. The thirty or so wooden coffins, which the Prince did not actually see being removed from the shaft, were probably gathered together from various sources by order of the local authorities and with the connivance of Mustapha Agha as a treat for the royal visitor. They were either 'salted' in the pit, recently found at Deir el-Medina, or possibly never went near the shaft. It is unclear whether the British consul was party to the deception or was one of its victims. Following the examination of the 'excavations' the royal party went on to the Ptolemaic temple and then to lunch beside another ruin, the Ramesseum. The Prince returned to England with twenty of the coffins which were distributed to various friends and museums throughout the country.

In 1858 the Egyptian Antiquities Service was formed under the leadership of Auguste Mariette (1821–81) to safeguard Egypt's heritage. From now on all excavations had to be authorized by the Service, and a portion of the antiquities had to remain in Egypt in the new Cairo Museum. Native excavators would be rewarded for any finds, but excavations without permission were frowned upon. In 1862 Mariette himself, and later his assistant Gabet, undertook brief excavations at Deir el-Medina. Needless to say, the authority of the Service was ignored or circumvented where possible by local diggers and antiquities dealers. In the 1870s a number of very fine papyri, faience vessels, canopic jars and *shabtis* inscribed with the names of the high priests of Amun of the Twenty-First Dynasty and their families began to appear on the market. The authorities at once realized that a major find had been made but the latter-day Theban tomb-robbers were unwilling to reveal their sources. Eventually in 1881, after severe questioning and family disagreements, Muhammad Abderrassul disclosed the location of a tomb near Deir el-Bahri which turned out to be the final resting-place of many New Kingdom pharaohs, who had been piously reburied in the Twenty-First Dynasty with the officers of the Deir el-Medina community in attendance. Now they were removed to Cairo to rest in the new museum. In 1898 the second royal cache was uncovered in the tomb of Amenhotpe II in the Valley of the Kings.

After the death of Mariette, the new director of the Service Gaston Maspero (1846–1916) was more generous in awarding concessions to excavate to both foreign and native diggers in return for all or part of the finds, or equivalent compensation. This policy bore fruit in Deir el-Medina, where the local residents were encouraged to clear many new tombs. On the evening of 1 February, an excited Egyptian presented himself to Maspero, who by chance was in Luxor, with the news that an intact tomb had been found in the valley of Deir el-Medina. Its wooden door was still in place. A foreman was immediately sent over to spend the night at the site in case cupidity got the better of the discoverers. In the morning Maspero crossed the river with a party which included the Spaniard Eduardo Toda (1852–1941), who made the most detailed notes of the discovery, although even these are by modern standards woefully inadequate. The tomb proved to be that of the workman Sennedjem, who flourished at the beginning of the Nineteenth Dynasty. His mummy, coffins and funerary equipment were recovered, as well as those of his wife Iineferti, his son Khons, his daughter-in-law Tameket, and a lady Isis who may have been a granddaughter or a daughter-in-law, or both if she married her uncle. Coffins and funerary objects of other members of the family were also found. The tomb had evidently been used for two generations of family burials. The objects were all taken to Cairo, but were unfortunately dispersed before adequate documentation was compiled. Sennedjem and his wife who had lain side by side for millenia were rudely divorced, as were their son Khons and his wife Tameket. Iineferti and her son Khons were awarded to the Metropolitan Museum of Art in New York, where their coffins now rest. Their mummies, however, were transferred to the Peabody Museum in Cambridge, Massachusetts. Tameket journeyed to the Berlin Museum, while her father-in-law Sennedjem remained behind in Cairo. Some of the minor finds were also kept in Cairo but others were scattered to Paris, Copenhagen, and Moscow.

Meanwhile the study and publication of the monuments of Deir el-Medina in European collections had begun. A large selection of the Turin

95 *The burial chamber in the tomb of Sennedjem. Relatives are shown in the wall-paintings; at the rear Sennedjem and his wife appear at work in the fields of paradise.*

papyri and the British Museum papyri were edited in the 1860s and 1870s. In 1880 and 1881 Maspero published many of the stelae in Turin with references to those in other collections. The early scholars did not at first recognize the true nature of the titles of the tomb workers. The most common title was literally translated as 'servant in the Place of Truth' and interpreted as reference to a judge in a court of law. The translation of 'judge' continued to be used by some until 1909. It was recognized before then that the servants must have been connected with the necropolis but it was assumed that they were mortuary priests and officials connected with the mortuary cults of the kings buried on the west bank of the Nile opposite Thebes.

The era of scientific excavations began with the work of Flinders Petrie (1853–1942) in the Delta in the 1880s and 1890s. Full-scale excavations began in the valley of Deir el-Medina in 1905 under the supervision of Ernesto Schiaparelli (1856–1928), curator of the Egyptian Museum, Turin. He was naturally interested in a site from which a large proportion of his museum's collection had originated, through the Drovetti collection. He dug in the valley in 1905, 1906 and 1909, and was rewarded with the discovery of the intact tomb of the foreman Kha, the contents of which are now one of the most important displays in the Turin Museum. Schiaparelli also uncovered many stelae, offering-tables and ostraca, some in a fragmentary condition. One highly interesting find was the left jamb of a small shrine, the rest of which had left Thebes in 1818 in the Belmore collection and was now in the British Museum. At the same time excavations in the Valley of the Queens by Schiaparelli and in the Valley of the Kings by Howard Carter (1874–1939) uncovered more traces of the workmen, notably in the form of ostraca. Repairs had been made to the Ptolemaic temple in the late nineteenth century, but from 1909 to 1912 Emile Baraize (1874–1952), an architect employed by the Egyptian Antiquities Service, carried out an extensive reconstruction, during which he found more traces of the earlier inhabitants of the site. In 1913 the Berlin Museum under Georg Möller (1876–1921) initiated further excavations in Deir el-Medina, but these were discontinued due to the outbreak of the First World War.

The final campaign, if anything can ever be said to be final in Egyptian archaeology, was undertaken by the French Institute of Oriental Archaeology in a series of extensive excavations stretching over thirty years and not yet finally completed. Work was begun in 1917, but the main excavations were carried out by the indefatigable Bernard Bruyère (1879–1971), who started off in the valley in 1922 and continued, with minor interruptions for such distractions as the Second World War, until 1951. He undertook to clear the village, the tombs and the surrounding area systematically. He was rewarded with an outstanding variety and richness of finds. A small number of early tombs were discovered intact. However, his greatest find was a large pit; although its original purpose is not clear, it was filled with thousands of ostraca which reflect the daily life of the inhabitants of the village. He also unearthed a number of important papyri. Unfortunately, his success encouraged illicit excavations on the site. As a result of these, a large number of ostraca and papyri appeared on the antiquities market and eventually found their way to various museums. These documents include the famous Sinuhe ostracon, the Chester Beatty papyri, part of the Naunakhte archive and sundry collections of ostraca. Bruyère published quick detailed preliminary reports on his excavations, so that scholars were able to study many of the finds without the long delays experienced in many other excavations. An ambitious plan was inaugurated to publish all the finds and the tombs in detail, and this is still in progress. A vast amount of documentary material consisting of literary and non-literary ostraca, papyri, figured ostraca, jar inscriptions and *shabtis* has appeared, and more catalogues remain to be completed. Many tombs have been published in photographs and line-drawings, but more still have to

96 (above)
*Schiaparelli's excavations
(1906). The workmen
carry reed baskets which
were used to remove the
excess earth and stone
from the excavations.*
97 (left) *The objects
from the tomb of Kha are
carefully carried out of
the Valley of Deir
el-Medina on their way
to the museum in Turin
during Schiaparelli's
excavations in 1906.*

98 (above) *Bruyère's excavations. The director, on the left, takes a break in the Valley with two of his closest collaborators, Georges Posener (centre), who published the literary ostraca, and Jaroslav Černý (right), who edited the non-literary ostraca.*

99 (below) *The Chester Beatty Papyrus No. I. This magnificent papyrus, which contains the* Contendings of Horus and Seth, *was discovered in a large roll which had to be carefully unrolled for the text to be examined.*

100 *Professor Černý at Deir el-Medina in 1970. It is fitting that this last picture of the scholar who devoted his life to unravelling the secrets of Deir el-Medina should be have been taken in front of his beloved village.*

be done. This task now has a new urgency, due to the deterioration of those tombs exposed to the elements after being buried for centuries.

The publication of the non-literary ostraca was chiefly the work of the noted Czech Egyptologist Jaroslav Černý (1898–1970), who in later years made his home in Britain, where he filled the chair of Egyptology at Oxford with great distinction. He joined Bruyère's team as a young man in 1925 and devoted the greater part of his career to unravelling the history of the community. In 1929 he firmly established that the inhabitants of Deir el-Medina were royal workmen, who constructed the royal tombs in the Valley of the Kings. He deciphered countless thousands of ostraca and papyri which recorded the daily activities of these workers and was instrumental in the publication of most of these accounts. In his later years he combed the cliffs of the west bank at Thebes recording the jottings or graffiti which the workmen had left behind. He intended to write a detailed history of the community and the Valley of the Kings, but unfortunately his sudden death intervened. Only a portion of the proposed history was ever completed. Even incomplete, together with his earlier works on Deir el-Medina, it remains the foundation on which all future students of the Deir el-Medina community must build. Every study of that village is a monument to his scholarship and his memory.

List of the Principal Kings

Overlapping dates usually indicate coregencies. All dates given are approximate.

FIRST DYNASTY
c. 3100–2890 BC

Narmer (Menes)
Aha
Djer
Djet (Uadji)
Den (Udimu)
Anedjib
Semerkhet
Qaa

SECOND DYNASTY
c. 2890–2686 BC

Hotepsekhemwy
Raneb
Nynetjer
Peribsen
Khasekhem (Khasekhemwy)

THIRD DYNASTY
c. 2686–2613 BC

Sanakhte
Djoser
Sekhemkhet
Khaba
Huni

FOURTH DYNASTY
c. 2613–2494 BC

Sneferu
Khufu (Cheops)
Redjedef
Khafre (Chephren)
Menkaure (Mycerinus)
Shepseskaf

FIFTH DYNASTY
c. 2494–2345 BC

Userkaf
Sahure
Neferirkare Kakai
Shepseskare Isi
Neferefre
Nyuserre
Menkauhor Akauhor
Djedkare Isesi
Unas

SIXTH DYNASTY
c. 2345–2181 BC

Teti
Userkare
Meryre Pepi I
Merenre Nemtyemsaf
Neferkare Pepi II

SEVENTH DYNASTY
c. 2181–2173 BC

EIGHTH DYNASTY
c. 2173–2160 BC

NINTH DYNASTY
c. 2160–2130 BC

Meryibre Khety I
Nebkaure Khety II

TENTH DYNASTY
c. 2130–2040 BC

Wahkare Khety III
Merykare

List of the Principal Kings

ELEVENTH DYNASTY
c. 2133–1991 BC

Tepya Mentuhotpe I
Sehertowy Inyotef I
Wahankh Inyotef II
Nakhtnebtepnefer Inyotef III
Nebhepetre Mentuhotpe II
Sankhkare Mentuhotpe III
Nebtowyre Mentuhotpe IV

TWELFTH DYNASTY
c. 1991–1786 BC

Sehetepibre Amenemhat I
1991–1962 BC
Kheperkare Senwosret I (Sesostris)
1971–1928 BC
Nubkaure Amenemhat II
1929–1895 BC
Khakheperre Senwosret II
1897–1878 BC
Khakaure Senwosret III
1878–1843 BC
Nymare Amenemhat III
1842–1797 BC
Makherure Amenemhat IV
1798–1790 BC
Sobkkare Sobkneferu
1789–1786 BC

THIRTEENTH DYNASTY
c. 1786–1633 BC

Sekhemre Sewadjtowy Sobkhotpe III
Khasekhemre Neferhotep
Meryankhre Mentuhotpe

FOURTEENTH DYNASTY
c. 1786–1603 BC

FIFTEENTH DYNASTY
(Hyksos)
c. 1660–1552 BC

Mayebre Sheshi
Meruserre Yakubher
Seuserenre Khyan
Auserre Apop I
Aqenenre Apop II

SIXTEENTH DYNASTY
c. 1660–*c.* 1552 BC

SEVENTEENTH DYNASTY
c. 1660–1552 BC

Nubkheperre Inyotef VII
Senakhtenre Tao I, 'the Elder'
Seqenenre Tao II, 'the Brave'
Wadjkheperre Kamose

EIGHTEENTH DYNASTY
c. 1552–1295 BC

Nebpehtyre Ahmose I
1552–1527 BC
Djeserkare Amenhotpe I (Amenophis)
1527–1506 BC
Akheperkare Thutmose I
1506–1493 BC
Akheperenre Thutmose II
1493–1479 BC
Makare Hatshepsut
1479–1458 BC
Menkheperre Thutmose III
1479–1425 BC
Akheprure Amenhotpe II
1427–1401 BC
Menkheprure Thutmose IV
1401–1390 BC
Nebmare Amenhotpe III
1390–1352 BC
Neferkheprure Amenhotpe IV
(Akhenaten)
1352–1336 BC
Ankhkheprure Smenkhkare
1338–1336 BC
Nebkheprure Tutankhamun
1336–1327 BC
Kheperkheprure Ay
1327–1323 BC
Djeserkheprure Horemheb
1323–1295 BC

NINETEENTH DYNASTY
c. 1295–1188 BC

Menpehtyre Ramesses I
1295–1294 BC
Menmare Seti I
1294–1279 BC

Usermare Ramesses II
1279–1212 BC
Baenre Merenptah
1212–1202 BC
Menmire Amenmesse
1202–1199 BC
Userkheprure Seti II
1202–1196 BC
Akhenre Siptah
1196–1190 BC
Sitre Tewosret
1196–1188 BC

TWENTIETH DYNASTY
c. 1188–1069 BC

Userkhaure Sethnakhte
1188–1186 BC
Usermare-Meryamun Ramesses III
1186–1154 BC
Hiqmare Ramesses IV
1154–1148 BC
Usermare Ramesses V
1148–1144 BC
Nebmare Ramesses VI
1144–1136 BC
Usermare Ramesses VII
1136–1128 BC
Usermare Ramesses VIII
1128–1125 BC
Neferkare Ramesses IX
1125–1107 BC
Khepermare Ramesses X
1107–1098 BC
Menmare Ramesses XI
1098–1069 BC

TWENTY-FIRST DYNASTY
c. 1069–945 BC

At Tanis
Hedjkhepperre Nesbanebded (Smendes)
Akheperre Psusenne I
Usermare Amenemope
Netjerkheperre Siamun
Titkheprure Psusenne II

At Thebes (High Priests)
Herihor (temp. Ramesses XI)
Paiankh
Pinudjem I

Masaherta
Menkheperre
Pinudjem II

TWENTY-SECOND DYNASTY
(Libyan or Bubastite)
c. 945–715 BC

Hedjkheperre Sheshonq I
945–924 BC
Sekhemkheperre Osorkon I
924–889 BC
Usermare Takelot I
889–874 BC
Usermare Osorkon II
874–850 BC
Hedjkheperre Takelot II
850–825 BC
Usermare Sheshonq III
825–773 BC
Usermare Pami
773–767 BC
Akheperre Sheshonq V
767–730 BC
Akheperre Osorkon IV
730–715 BC

TWENTY-THIRD DYNASTY
c. 818–715 BC

Usermare Pedubast I
818–793 BC
Usermare Osorkon III
777–749 BC

TWENTY-FOURTH DYNASTY
c. 727–715 BC

Shepsesre Tefnakhte
Wahkare Bakenrenef (Bocchoris)

TWENTY-FIFTH DYNASTY
(Nubian or Kushite)
c. 747–656 BC

Piankhi (Piye)
747–716 BC
Neferkare Shabaka
716–702 BC

147

List of the Principal Kings

Djedkaure Shebitku
702–690 BC
Khunefertemre Taharqa
690–664 BC
Bakare Tanutamun
664–656 BC

TWENTY-SIXTH DYNASTY
(Saite)
664–525 BC

Wahibre Psamtik I
664–610 BC
Wehemibre Neko II
610–595 BC
Neferibre Psamtik II
595–589 BC
Haibre Wahibre (Apries)
589–570 BC
Khnemibre Ahmose II
570–526 BC
Ankhkaenre Psamtik III
526–525 BC

TWENTY-SEVENTH DYNASTY
(Persian)
525–404 BC

Cambyses
525–522 BC
Darius I
522–486 BC
Xerxes
486–465 BC
Artaxerxes I
465–424 BC
Darius II
424–405 BC
Artaxerxes II
405–359 BC

TWENTY-EIGHTH DYNASTY
404–399 BC

Amenirdis (Amyrtaeus)
404–399 BC

TWENTY-NINTH DYNASTY
399–380 BC

Baenre Neferud I
399–393 BC
Khnemmare Hagor
393–380 BC
Neferud II
380 BC

THIRTIETH DYNASTY
380–343 BC

Kheperkare Nekhtnebef (Nectanebo I)
380–362 BC
Irmantenre Djedhor (Teos)
362–360 BC
Snedjemibre Nekhtharheb
(Nectanebo II)
360–343 BC

PERSIAN KINGS
343–332 BC

Artaxerxes III Ochus
343–338 BC
Arses
338–336 BC
Darius III
336–332 BC

MACEDONIAN KINGS
332–305 BC

Alexander the Great
332–323 BC
Philip Arrhidaeus
323–317 BC
Alexander IV
317–305 BC

THE PTOLEMIES
305–30 BC

Ptolemy I Soter I
305–282 BC
Ptolemy II Philadelphus
284–246 BC

Ptolemy III Euergetes I
246–222 BC
Ptolemy IV Philopator
222–205 BC
Ptolemy V Epiphanes
205–180 BC
Ptolemy VI Philometor
180–145 BC
Ptolemy VII Neos Philopator
145 BC
Ptolemy VIII Euergetes II
170–116 BC

Ptolemy IX Soter II (Lathyros)
116–107 BC
Ptolemy X Alexander I
107–88 BC
Ptolemy IX Soter II (restored)
88–80 BC
Ptolemy XI Alexander II
80 BC
Ptolemy XII Neos Dionysos (Auletes)
80–51 BC
Cleopatra VII Philopator
51–30 BC

Bibliography

Allam, S. *Hieratische Ostraka und Papyri.* 2 vols. Tübingen, 1973.

Barns, J. W. B. *The Ashmolean Ostracon of Sinuhe.* Oxford, 1952.

Belzoni, G. *Narrative of the operations and recent discoveries within the pyramids, temples, tombs, and excavations in Egypt and Nubia.* London, 1822.

Bierbrier, M. L. *The Late New Kingdom in Egypt.* Warminster, 1975.

Bierbrier, M. L. 'Terms of Relationship at Deir el-Medina', *The Journal of Egyptian Archaeology* 66 (1980), pp. 100–107.

Blackman, A. M. 'Oracles in Ancient Egypt', *The Journal of Egyptian Archaeology* 12 (1926), pp. 176–185.

Bogoslovsky, E. S. 'Monuments and Documents from Dêr el-Medina in the Museums of the USSR,' *Vestnik Drevnii Istori* 119–125 (1972–73).

Botti, G. *L'Archivo Demotico da Deir el-Medineh.* Florence, 1967.

Botti, G. and Peet, T. E. *Il Giornale della necropoli di Tebe.* Turin, 1928.

The British Museum. *Hieroglyphic Texts from Egyptian Stelae* . . . Vols. 8–10. London, 1939–1982.

Bruyère, B. *Mert Seger à Deir el Médineh.* Cairo, 1930.

Bruyère, B. *Rapport sur les fouilles de Deir el Médineh.* 17 vols. Cairo, 1924–53.

Bruyère, B. *Le Tombe no. 1 de Sennedjem à Deir el Médineh.* Cairo, 1959.

Bruyère, B. *Tombes thébaines de Deir el Médineh à decoration monochrome.* Cairo, 1952.

Cailliaud, F. *Voyage à l'Oasis de Thèbes et dans les Déserts situés à l'Orient et à l'Occident de la Thébaide.* Paris, 1822–4.

Cailliaud, F. *Voyage à Meroé.* Paris, 1823–7.

Capart, J., Gardiner, A. H., and van de Walle, B. 'New Light on the Ramesside Tomb Robberies', *The Journal of Egyptian Archaeology* 22 (1936), pp. 169–193.

Černý, J. *The Cambridge Ancient History.* 3rd edn. Vol. II, part 2. Chapter XXXV. Cambridge, 1975.

Černý, J. *Catalogue des ostraca hiératiques non-littéraires de Deir el Médineh.* 6 vols. Cairo, 1937–1970.

Černý, J. *A Community of Workmen at Thebes in the Ramesside Period.* Cairo, 1973.

Černý, J. 'Le culte d'Amenophis Ier chez les ouvriers de la nécropole thébaine', *Bulletin de l'Institut français d'archéologie orientale* 27 (1927), pp. 159–203.

Černý, J. 'Egyptian Oracles' in R. Parker *A Saite oracle Papyrus from Thebes.* Providence, 1962.

Černý, J. *Egyptian Stelae in the Bankes Collection.* Oxford, 1958.

Černý, J. *Graffiti hiéroglyphiques et hiératiques de la nécropole thébaine.* Cairo, 1956.

Černý, J. 'L'identité des "serviteurs dans la Place de Vérité" et des ouvriers de la nécropole royale de Thèbes', *Revue de l'Égypte ancienne* 2 (1929), pp. 200–209.

Černý, J. *O·traca hiératiques.* Cairo, 1930–1935.

Černý, J. *Papyrus hiératiques de Deir el-Medineh.* Tome I. Cairo, 1978.

Černý, J. 'Papyrus Salt 124', *The Journal of Egyptian Archaeology* 15 (1929), pp. 243–258.

Černý, J. *Répertoire onomastique de Deir el Médineh.* Cairo, 1949.

Černý, J. 'Quelques ostraca hiératiques inédits de Thèbes au Musée du Caire', *Annales du Service des Antiquités d'Égypte* 27 (1927), pp. 183–210.

Černý, J. 'Studies in the Chronology of the Twenty-First Dynasty', *The Journal of Egyptian Archaeology* 32 (1946), pp. 24–30.

Černý, J. *The Valley of the Kings*. Cairo, 1973.

Černý, J. 'The Will of Naunakhte and the related documents', *The Journal of Egyptian Archaeology* 31 (1945), pp. 29–53.

Černý, J., and Gardiner, A. H. *Hieratic Ostraca*. Vol. I. Oxford, 1957.

Černý, J., and Sadek, A. A. *Graffiti de la Montagne thébaine*. Vols. III–IV. Cairo, 1970 ff.

Clère, J. J. 'Un monument de la réligion populaire de l'époque ramesside', *Revue d'Égyptologie* 27 (1975), pp. 70–77.

Curto, S. and Mancini, M. 'News of Kha' and Meryt', *The Journal of Egyptian Archaeology* 54 (1968), pp. 77–81.

Daressy, G. *Ostraca*. Cairo, 1901.

Dawson, W. R. and Uphill, E. P. *Who was who in Egyptology*. 2nd edn. London, 1972.

Della Monica, M. *La Classe ouvrière sous les Pharaons*. Paris, 1975.

Edgerton, W. 'The Strikes in Ramses III's Twenty-Ninth Year', *Journal of Near Eastern Studies* 10 (1951), pp. 137–145.

Edwards, I. E. S. 'Kenhikhopshef's Prophylactic Charm', *The Journal of Egyptian Archaeology* 54 (1968), pp. 155–160.

Gardiner, A. H. *The Chester Beatty Papyri*, No. I. London, 1931.

Gardiner, A. H. *Hieratic Papyri in the British Museum*. 3rd Series. London, 1935.

Gardiner, A. H. et al. *Theban Ostraca*. Oxford, 1913.

Grey, W. *Journal of a Visit to Egypt, Constantinople, the Crimea, Greece, etc. in the suite of the Prince and Princess of Wales*. London, 1869.

Gunn, B. 'The Religion of the Poor in Ancient Egypt', *The Journal of Egyptian Archaeology* 3 (1916), pp. 81–94.

Habachi, L. *Tavole d'offerta are e bacili da libagione*. Turin, 1977.

Halls, J. J. *The Life and Correspondence of Henry Salt, Esq*. London, 1834.

Hamilton, W. *Aegyptiaca*. London, 1809.

Hawkins, E. *Tablets and Other Egyptian Monuments from the Collection of the Earl of Belmore*. London, 1843.

Hayes, W. C. *The Scepter of Egypt*. Vol. 2. Cambridge, Mass., 1959.

Holscher, U. *The Excavations of Medinet Habu*. Vol. V. Chicago, 1954.

Janssen, J. J. *Commodity Prices from the Ramessid Period*. Leiden, 1975.

Janssen, J. J. 'Khaemtore, a well-to-do Workman', *Oudheidkundige Mededelingen uit het Rijksmuseum van Oudheden te Leiden* LVIII (1977), pp. 221–232.

Janssen, J. J. 'Absence from work by the necropolis workmen of Thebes'. *Studien zur Altägyptischen Kultur* 8 (1980), pp. 127–152.

Jollois, J. B. P. and Devilliers, R.E. 'Description générale de Thèbes'. *Description de l'Égypte*. Tome 2. Paris, 1821.

Kitchen, K. A. *The Third Intermediate Period in Egypt*. Warminster, 1973.

Lichtheim, M. *Ancient Egyptian Literature*. Vol. II. Berkeley, 1976.

López, J. *Ostraca Ieratici*. Turin, 1978–80.

Maspero, G. 'Rapport sur une mission en Italie', *Recueil de travaux rélatifs à la philologie et à l'archéologie égyptiennes et assyriennes* 2 (1880), pp. 159–99.

Maystre, C. *La Tombe de Nebenmât*. Cairo, 1936.

Moss, R. B. 'An Egyptian Statuette in Malta', *The Journal of Egyptian Archaeology* 35 (1949), pp. 132–134.

Omlin, J. *Der Papyrus 55001 und seine satirisch-erotischen Zeichnungen und Inschriften*. Turin, 1973.

Peck, W. H. *Drawings from Ancient Egypt*. London, 1978.

Peet, T. E. *The Great Tomb-robberies of the Twentieth Egyptian Dynasty*. Oxford, 1930.

Peet, T. E. and Woolley, C. L. *The*

Bibliography

City of Akhenaten. Vol. I. London, 1923.

Pestman, P. W. *Marriage and Matrimonial Property in Ancient Egypt*. Leiden, 1961.

Petrie, W. M. F. *Illahun, Kahun, and Gurob*. London, 1891.

Petrie, W. M. F. *Pyramids and Temples of Gizeh*. London, 1883.

Pleyte, W. and Rossi, F. *Papyrus de Turin*. Leiden, 1869–76.

Pococke, R. *A Description of the East*. Vol. I. London, 1743.

Porter, B. and Moss, R. *Topographical Bibliography of Ancient Egyptian Hieroglyphic Texts, Reliefs, and Paintings*. 2nd edn. Vols I and II. Oxford, 1960–72.

Posener, G. *Catalogue des ostraca hiératiques littéraires de Deir el-Médineh*. 3 vols. Cairo, 1938–78.

Pestman, P. W. and Janssen, J. 'Burial and inheritance in the community of the Necropolis Workmen at Thebes', *Journal of the Economic and Social History of the Orient* XI (1968), pp. 137–170.

Richardson, R. *Travels along the Mediterranean and parts adjacent, in company with the Earl of Belmore, during years 1816, 1817, and 1818*. London, 1822.

Richter, O. F. von *Wallfahrten im Morgenlande*. Berlin, 1822.

Russell, W. H. *A Diary in the East during the Tour of the Prince and Princess of Wales*. London, 1869.

Sauneron, S. *Catalogue des ostraca hiératiques non littéraires de Deir el Médineh*. Cairo, 1959.

Schiaparelli, E. *Relazione sui lavori della missione archeologica italiana in Egitto (anni 1903–1920). Volume secundo: La Tomba intatta dell' architetto Cha nella necropoli di Tebe*. Turin, 1927.

Simpson, W. K. (ed.) *The Literature of Ancient Egypt*. New Haven, 1972.

Sonnini de Manoncour, C. *Voyage dans la Haute et Basse Égypte*. Paris, 1799.

Spiegelberg, W. *Ägyptische und andere Graffiti aus der Thebanischen Nekropolis*. Heidelberg, 1921.

Théodorides, A. 'Le droit matrimonial dans l'Égypte pharaonique', *Revue internationale des Droits de l'Antiquité* 3e série, 23 (1976), pp. 15–55.

Théodorides, A. 'Les ouvriers "magistrats" en Égypte à l'Époque Ramesside', *Revue internationale des Droits de l'Antiquité* 3e serie, 16 (1969), pp. 103–188.

Toda, E. 'La Decouverte et l'Inventaire du tombeau de Sen-nezem', *Annales du Service des Antiquités de l'Égypte* 20 (1920), pp. 145–60.

Tosi, M. and Roccati, A. *Stele e altre epigrafi di Deir el Medina*. Turin, 1972.

Valbelle, D. *Catalogue des Poids à inscriptions hiératiques de Deir el-Médineh*. Cairo, 1977.

Valbelle, D. *Ouchebtis de Deir el-Médineh*. Cairo, 1972.

Valbelle, D. *La Tombe de Hay à Deir el-Médineh (No. 267)*. Cairo, 1975

Vandier, J. *La Tombe de Nefer-abou*. Cairo, 1935.

Vandier d'Abbadie, J. *Catalogue des ostraca figurés de Deir el Médineh*. 2 vols. Cairo, 1936–59.

Vandier d'Abbadie, J. and Jourdain, G. *Deux Tombes de Deir el Médineh*. Cairo, 1939.

Wente, E. *Late Ramesside Letters*. Chicago, 1966.

Wild, H. *La Tombe de Nefer·hotep (I) et Neb·nefer à Deir el Médina* [No. 6]. II. Cairo, 1979.

Wilkinson, J. G. *Topography of Thebes and General View of Egypt*. London, 1835.

Winlock, H. E. and Crum, W. E. *The Monastery of Epiphanius at Thebes*. I. New York, 1926.

Zivie, A.-P. *La Tombe de Pached à Deir el-Médineh*. Cairo, 1979.

Sources of the Illustrations

The photos were provided by the institutions who own the objects illustrated, except where indicated. The author and publishers wish to thank the copyright holders for permission to reproduce the photographs. The drawings are by Mrs C. Barratt.

1 Museo Egizio, Turin (Turin Sup. n. 6127).
2 Photo courtesy of the Museum of Fine Arts, Boston, Department of Egyptian Antiquities.
3 British Museum, London, Department of Egyptian Antiquities (BM EA 64578, 67784, 33940).
4 British Museum, London, Department of Egyptian Antiquities (BM EA 37993).
5 Photo by Egyptian Expedition, Metropolitan Museum of Art, New York.
6 Photo courtesy of Dr R. J. Demarée.
7, 8, 9 Reproduced from E. Schiaparelli *La Tomba Intatta dell' architetto Cha* (Turin, 1927), by courtesy of the Museo Egizio, Turin.
10 Photo courtesy of the Museo Egizio, Turin.
11 Reproduced from T. E. Peet and C. L. Woolley *The City of Akhenaten Part I* (London, 1923), pl. XVI; by courtesy of the Egypt Exploration Society, London.
12 Photo courtesy of the Egypt Exploration Society, London.
13 Photo courtesy of Mr T. G. H. James.
14 British Museum, London, Department of Egyptian Antiquities (BM EA 265).
15 Photo courtesy of the Griffith Institute, Ashmolean Museum, Oxford.
16 British Museum, London, Department of Egyptian Antiquities (BM EA 1516).
17 Manchester Museum, University of Manchester (4588).
18 Manchester Museum, University of Manchester (1759): photo courtesy of Dr A. J. Spencer.
19, 20 British Museum, London, Department of Egyptian Antiquities (BM EA 10683).
21 British Museum, London, Department of Egyptian Antiquities (BM EA 35630).
22 Photo courtesy of Dr R. J. Demarée.
23 British Museum, London, Department of Egyptian Antiquities (BM EA 5635).
24 Photo courtesy of British Museum, Department of Egyptian Antiquities.
25 British Museum, London, Department of Egyptian Antiquities (BM EA 50722).
27 Museo Egizio, Turin (Turin n. 1885).
28 Fitzwilliam Museum, Cambridge (EGA 4324a.1943).
29, 30, 31, 32 Photos by Egypt Expedition, Metropolitan Museum of Art, New York.
33 Photo courtesy of Dr R. J. Demarée.
34 British Museum, London, Department of Egyptian Antiquities (BM EA 5634).
35 Photo by Egypt Expedition, Metropolitan Museum of Art, New York.
36 Photo courtesy of Mrs A. Allott and family.
38 British Museum, London, Department of Egyptian Antiquities (BM EA 305).
39 Manchester Museum, University of Manchester (5966).
40 British Museum, London, Department of Egyptian Antiquities (BM EA 1754).

Sources of the Illustrations

41 Photo courtesy of Dr R. J.
Demarée.
42 Metropolitan Museum of Art, New
York (86.1.5 A–C).
43 Metropolitan Museum of Art, New
York (47.139 A, B).
44 British Museum, London,
Department of Egyptian Antiquities
(BM EA 9955).
45 Reproduced from E. Schiaparelli
La Tomba Intatta dell' architetta Cha
(Turin, 1927), by courtesy of the
Museo Egizio, Turin.
46 Photo courtesy of Mr T. G. H.
James.
48 Photo courtesy of the Griffith
Institute, Ashmolean Museum,
Oxford.
49 British Museum, London,
Department of Egyptian Antiquities
(BM EA 63783).
50 British Museum, London,
Department of Egyptian Antiquities
(BM EA 8506).
51 Photo courtesy of the Griffith
Institute, Ashmolean Museum,
Oxford.
52 Museo Egizio, Turin (Turin
Papyrus 55001).
53 Photo courtesy of the Griffith
Institute, Ashmolean Museum,
Oxford.
54 British Museum, London,
Department of Egyptian Antiquities
(BM EA 68539).
55 Ägyptisches Museum, Berlin
(21442).
56 Egyptian Museum, Cairo (12–11/
16–5).
57 British Museum, London,
Department of Egyptian Antiquities
(BM EA 10683).
58 Ashmolean Museum, Oxford.
59 Photo courtesy of the French
Institute of Archaeology, Cairo.
60 British Museum, London,
Department of Egyptian Antiquities
(BM EA 316).
61 Museo Egizio, Turin (Turin n.
3032).
62 British Museum, London,
Department of Egyptian Antiquities
(BM EA 8508).

63 British Museum, London,
Department of Egyptian Antiquities
(BM EA 1466).
64 Photo courtesy of Dr R. J. Demarée.
65 British Museum, London,
Department of Egyptian Antiquities
(BM EA 191).
66 Museo Egizio, Turin (Turin n.
1369).
67 Museo Egizio, Turin (Turin n.
1372).
68 Kestner Museum, Hanover (2936);
photo courtesy of Prof. Dr and
Mrs Munro.
69 British Museum, London,
Department of Egyptian Antiquities
(BM EA 270).
70 British Museum, London,
Department of Egyptian Antiquities
(BM EA 444).
71 British Museum, London,
Department of Egyptian Antiquities
(BM EA 589).
72 Reproduced by courtesy of the
Chester Beatty Library, Dublin.
73 British Museum, London,
Department of Egyptian Antiquities
(BM EA 278).
74 Ashmolean Museum, Oxford (P
Ashmolean Museum 1945.97).
75 British Museum, London,
Department of Egyptian Antiquities
(BM EA 65930).
76 British Museum, London,
Department of Egyptian Antiquities
(BM EA 10055).
77 British Museum, London,
Department of Egyptian Antiquities
(BM EA 272).
78 Photo courtesy of Dr R. J.
Demarée.
79 British Museum, London,
Department of Egyptian Antiquities
(BM EA 10221).
80, 81 Photos courtesy of the Oriental
Institute, University of Chicago.
82 British Museum, London,
Department of Egyptian Antiquities
(BM EA 10375).
83, 84 Photos courtesy of the French
Institute of Archaeology, Cairo.
85 British Museum, London,
Department of Egyptian Antiquities

(BM EA 32).

86 Reproduced from Sonnini de Manoncour *Travels in Upper and Lower Egypt* (London, 1800) pl. XVIII.

87 Reproduced from the *Journal of Egyptian Archaeology* 35 (1949) pl. XIII by courtesy of Miss R. Moss.

88 Fitzwilliam Museum, Cambridge (E191.1932).

89 Reproduced from E. Hawkins, *Tablets and other Egyptian Monuments from the Collections of the Earl of Belmore, now desposited in the British Museum* (London, 1843).

90 British Library, London, Department of Manuscripts (MSS Add 29843).

91 Reproduced by courtesy of His Grace the Duke of Hamilton; photo courtesy of Mr S. Reid, Strathclyde County Park.

92 British Museum, London, Department of Egyptian Antiquities (BM EA 5612).

93 Reproduced from R. Lepsius, *Denkmäler aus Aegypten und Aethiopien*, Text iii (Leipzig, 1910) p. 295.

94 Brussels M.R.A.H. (E6879): photo reproduced by courtesy of A.C.L. Brussels.

95 Photo by Egypt Expedition, Metropolitan Museum of Art, New York.

96, 97 Reproduced from E. Schiaparelli *La Tomba Intatta dell' architetta Cha* (Turin, 1927), by courtesy of the Museo Egizio, Turin.

98 Photo courtesy of Mrs A. Allott and family.

99 Reproduced by courtesy of the Chester Beatty Library, Dublin.

100 Photo courtesy of Mrs A. Allott and family.

Index

Figures in roman refer to page numbers and figures in *italics* to illustrations

Index

Index

Index